Is Your Mind Shackle Free

This is not a Riddle: This is some Knowledge to Stimulate your Mind and Make you Think. Ask Yourself, is my Mind Shackle Free?

Ryan Strickland

authorHOUSE®

AuthorHouse™
1663 Liberty Drive, Suite 200
Bloomington, IN 47403
www.authorhouse.com
Phone: 1-800-839-8640

First published by AuthorHouse 6/5/2008

ISBN: 978-1-4343-3667-5 (sc)

Library of Congress Control Number: 2007906982

Printed in the United States of America
Bloomington, Indiana

This book is printed on acid-free paper.

CONTENTS

Disclosure

Author House is merely the publishing company and does not have any sharing opinions either way with the author of "Is Your Mind Shackle Free?"

Furthermore, I believe in God and speak of God throughout my book. However, there are still some terms I use to make specific points, which may be offensive to some. I have great respect to all mankind, to all religions, and mean no disrespect to anyone.

There are also small usages of slang to make my point more clear.

Some of you may ask, "What gives you the right to write this book or any book for that matter, especially when you do not hold a traditional degree?" These same people have borrowed from my book and not given me the credit. **The truth is here! Therefore, this is for the record.**

I'd like to say that I have a degree in life, which consists of my life's hardships, lessons, and experiences. As we know, there are many ways of learning. Have you ever heard someone say: "that person is book smart, but has no common sense?" The other way this is put is: "wow, book smart, but no street smarts." Another is: "street smarts and not a lick of book smarts." I like to say I am blessed with a little bit of both. I have taken enough from both sides to survive in my lifestyle which I have chosen to live. Now, I am trying to expand my lifestyle. Part of my expansion is going back to school to receive a traditional degree. It is difficult to live a good life without both of these worlds. I'm not saying it's impossible. I'm just saying, the world along with the technology is rapidly changing, and this is going to make things a bit more challenging. If we want to continue to survive, we must also change. Last but not least, I am an American; this alone gives me the right to express myself. George Washington once said: "If freedom of speech is taken away, then dumb and silent we shall be lead like sheep to the slaughter."

You have this freedom to express yourself due to many years of bloodshed. Use it, or it will be taken away.

Warning: Do not take this as an insult. Some of the material is very straight forward, and harsh; as is our life's journey at times. This is coming from someone who looks just like you; and has shared a lot of your pain, and struggles. Hell, I'm still in the struggle. I am tired of the struggle. While reading my book, you may experience pain, anger, sadness, joy, and some frustration. Just keep reading. I know I am not alone and this is why I've placed this journey on the billboard for the world to see. I'm just hoping, that when finished reading my book, the most memorable emotion you feel is *motivation*. This, along with all of the other emotions, is what I want you to use to get out of your slump. Whether you are in one or not, use it to reach out to someone

else and pull them up, instead of pulling them down. By doing so, we can truly regain our rightful and respectable place in life.

Thank you,

Enjoy,
Peace,
Ryan E. Strickland

Preface

I Was Created In A Cocoon!

I have been in a cocoon since the day of my birth. As soon as I was born I was turned upside down and slapped on my ass. Then, I was turned right side up, cleaned up and embraced. I take this to be my first lesson on life. What should my interpretation be, you ask? Life is going to be painful, but you should clean yourself up and embrace it. I was learning how to communicate. When I cried, I was fed or changed. My interpretation is, in life, communication is greatly needed in order for me to get my needs met, or my point across. I was learning how to crawl. My interpretation is, in life, I must first build a foundation. I then learned how to stand. My interpretation is, in life, balance is needed and is very important. I then learned how to walk. My interpretation is, in life, you are going to fall, but in order to learn and succeed you have to pick yourself up and continue to try. If I was to do something, I learned rather quickly whether it was a good thing or a bad thing, depending on the outcome. If it was good, I received praise or some other sort of reward. If I did something bad, I received some type of reprimand. What was my interpretation here? Life sometimes rewards you for good doings and will also punish you for your bad.

These are a few of the basic fundamentals that we are taught even before we face the world. This is my interpretation of life; it will be different for all of us. Each of us will encounter a cocoon stage throughout our lives; however, the outcome of how we evolve depends on you.

"IF WE AS BLACK PEOPLE ACCEPT EACH OTHER, WE WON'T HAVE TO WORRY ABOUT OTHER RACES ACCEPTING US."

This book is very simple, with issues that, in my opinion, are also simple, but we as humans make them complex. I am approaching these issues from a (strickly) personal perspective. In order to support my beliefs, I'll give you my reasons why, we as Black people, act the way we do toward one another. I offer some questions, explanations, opinions, observations, along with my life experiences and research. I offer some of my solutions, which are just suggestions. We, who have come from a long generation of slavery, have had our minds altered. The Proclamation was issued September 22, 1862 and placed into effect January 1, 1863 by President Abraham Lincoln, which states that all slaves are to be free. Yet, in the year 2008, long after the physical aspect of slavery is gone, we are still haunted by the mental aspects of slavery. Doctors have said, for some time now, that psychological abuse will affect a person much longer than physical abuse. For anyone who thinks this affects only the Black people of the world, please think again. This affects us all. Just take a look around you. Not only does Black America have issues, Americans have issues. Even so, we can still change this situation. We must first address the problems that lay in front of us. I feel we must find a solution and implement a functional plan. We can better America. We should not have to search or wait for another leader to be born. We can all be leaders or at least we can mold ourselves to become leaders. This is 2008 and the choice is ours and has been for sometime. So I ask you this, why put this weight on one person's shoulders when we were all born with two? We would be much better off as Americans; if we recognize and solve our own problems first before we help others solve theirs.

Here is a list of stimulating questions:

What would be the best way to keep a race of people from making progress?

1. Psychological Slavery?
2. Keeping them uneducated?
3. Keeping them in the low income bracket and in debt?
4. **Would drugs cause them to become immobilized? (Selling or Using)**
5. How does Racial Profiling fit in?
6. **Could segregation within one's race prove beneficial?**
7. Would breaking up the family count?
8. Would keeping them felons or pushing them to become felons play a part?
9. Does incarceration of the male figure help?
10. **How would the reversal of roles in the homes affect the outcome of the relationships?**
11. If a woman is more independent and more educated than the man, would this make her a single parent for life?
12. Can we truly seek opportunity, or are we still some sort of hidden opportunity?

Here are some questions to take into consideration along with this:

Eugene Thomas is a very successful businessman from Chicago. He is a highly ranked entrepreneur in Chicago, the United States and possibly even the World. He once said "Other minorities came to America seeking opportunity; Black people were brought to America as the opportunity."

I feel this is a very powerful and wise statement that we should hear, absorb, and value the truth it brings forward. Now, we need to come up with a solution that will help better our race indefinitely.

We as Black/African Americans have been enslaved physically and psychologically for many years. I must also say that we have been trained well. The government does not want to accept any liability for their role in enslaving us. Although the physical shackles are no longer present, it is very obvious that the psychological shackles are. Beyond any doubt, these shackles are still incredibly strong wounding us all today. Have you ever seen a large elephant being held by a small stake in the ground? If you were to see this at the beginning you would have witnessed a small elephant being held with a large stake. As the elephant grew larger the restraints get smaller. This technique could be considered *Ironic* or *Genius* depending on how you look at it.

Our ancestors were beaten, tortured, burned, raped, and ripped apart, hanged/lynched, slaughtered as well as massacred. Our leaders were taunted and persecuted; some were considered trouble makers and in some cases they were even *assassinated*. As America grew, the physical shackles disappeared; however, the psychological shackles still linger even to this day. If you think about it, there really is no difference between the elephant's torture and the torture of Black/African Americans. Please take a moment of your time to give this some thought. The only distinction between the two is the elephant's torture was milder, yet the effect is still long lasting. If you do not feel this sort of distress has a long term effect on a race of people, I ask you to reconsider. If the government accepted responsibility for their actions, we as Black/African Americans could accept responsibility for ours. We cannot heal ourselves without help. America has trained us to fail by providing us with a poor education. In return, it wants to complain if we do not work or if some of us may commit crimes. Reparation can come in many forms. If we really want our America to be *truly grand*, then we should start correcting our mistakes. I do believe, or should I say, need to believe, we are all on the same page when I say "Slavery was a mistake." Slavery created the *"Psychological Slave,"* which has been very detrimental to all Americans. More importantly, I think slavery has, without doubt, "INFECTED US ALL." Please think about this. With this in mind, I recommend we start "Operation Reversal." Let's call it "THE REVERSAL OF THE PSYCHOLOGICAL SLAVE." Doesn't that have a nice ring to it? We are Americans, as well as humans. Can we please be treated and counted as such? When will this Begin?

Foreword/Dedications

Thank you everyone who have made some sort of sacrifice, whether it was knowingly or unknowingly, for our rights in America and the world. It was strongly put on my heart to write this. I hope and pray that this will be read, digested, well received, and understood to the utmost. Please consider all I'm saying with an open mind. Absorb the information before you try to find fault and rip me apart. I did not write this to put anyone down or to offend anyone. Although it seems that no matter what we do, someone always gets offended. This is what I see and have experienced firsthand. I recognize that I am not alone. All of our voices can be heard. When the torch is passed we must accept the torch with proud honor and not fear. Reason being, it is the responsibility of all to make a difference in this world. We are obligated to try to improve our people and the world. It does not matter how young or old we are. It is never too soon nor too late. You must believe that.

To all of the strong Black /African Americans, who are in the limelight, we only see the glamorous side of your career. What about the other side, which is rarely spoken of anymore. For example, being able to perform for Tha-Man but not being allowed to eat in the same room as Tha-Man. Thank you for the degrading moments you endured alone to help pave the way for your people. I am deeply sorry for all the struggles you went through and are still going through today. It is mortifying to think about what you have tolerated just so we can share the so called "American Dream." Thank you again! Continue to stay strong and keep doing what you do best! Although you may have felt alone, you were truly never alone. God was always present with you!

To every brother who keeps pushing toward your goals, with the endeavor of reaching your full potential; you are not alone! I know that you are tired of hearing this, but your time is coming soon. Same goes for the brother who is sitting on that couch smoking a blunt, thinking that no matter what he does, things will never change. That is the weed talking, so put it down and get up off that couch. Your voice does matter and can be heard, not only by you, but by others as well.

To my biological and step parents, as well as my entire family, it doesn't matter if we are related by blood or not, God blessed us all when he allowed us to cross each other's paths. We should be thankful for being in good company. To everyone that is close to me in my life, Thank you.

This is for all of the Black/African Americans who are making a difference in their communities by having their own businesses. Thank you for breaking through doors and other obstacles allowing a smoother path for the rest of us. Thank you for showing us that the "SKY IS THE LIMIT", NOT "THE LIMIT IS THE SKY!" In other words, thank you for encouraging us to be successful. Peace!

To a real brother, Mr. Vernon (aka Mr. V.I.P.), thank you for your inspirational insight and moral support. Thank you for taking time to share your knowledge in this area and for challenging my mind to bring me to another level. May you reach all of your goals and dreams! Also may God continue to send blessings your way! Peace!

Mr. Edward Smith Thank you, for your guidance, wisdom and moral support from an elderly brother's perspective, or better yet, an OG's point of view. May you continue to receive blessings and much success on your book! Peace!

Linda, (aka DJ Budda Fly), I'd like to give you this special thank you even though you don't believe this will really help nor do you really believe in me. We are still cool and I hope you are wrong, this time. With that being said, thank you for passing me the knowledge that opened my mind and eyes to a different world which gave me the courage and strength to write this book. Much love! Peace and God bless! P.S. our birthdays are a blessing from God; you were a blessing to your parents. Therefore, you should start celebrating your birthday again.

To the Pastor of A.M.E. Murph Community Church, Pastor T. Nelson, thank you. You believed me in the end when I enlightened you about Willie Lynch, in spite of others who did not. Willie Lynch was a real person. We did a search which found him to be so, along with his family history. More importantly, you gave me credit for bringing Willie Lynch to your attention. I would also like to thank you for taking it a step further and preaching a sermon on it. In addition, I'd like to give you and your husband Wilber a very special thank you for helping out my niece Tha-Sha. Even though my mother and step-father raised her, the two of you managed to embrace Tha-Sha and made her an addition to your family as if she was your own. You were there for her at times when we were not. Thank you for that! Stay strong, stay blessed. Peace!

Anthony and Jerry, I'd like to thank you for keeping a brother in gas money while attending college. I know you thought I forgot. Another thing, continue to keep the Black/African American family together. You are proud husbands and fathers. The two of you brothers truly beat all odds.

Thank you, J.J., for helping a brother out in my time of need. Thank you for being a real brother and for not having the crabby mentality.

Good looking out to another true brother, Travis and family. Thank you for keeping it real and being supportive in a time of need. Stay strong and continue to keep your family tight.

Thank you, to two sisters Michelle and Monica, good looking out. Stay strong and continue to keep it real. Peace!

To a young brother, SSG Mitchell, Thank you for keeping it real and for opening up your doors when a brother needed a helping hand.

To all of the food service specialists (92G/94B's) you are real soldiers even though you are very much underrated. We all know that you are the true backbone of the Army. You cannot work if you are hungry. May all of the Soldiers stay strong, blessed and safe!

To Ava, a local superstar in the community, who has decided to dedicate her time giving back to her people, thank you (Major Breakthrough). Keep up the outstanding work and stay strong. I will do my best to have your back and support you in your positive efforts. Call me. Peace! Stay blessed!

Here is a little something, something, for the mother of my children, Meiling. Although we both know you can be difficult and we don't always see eye to eye on things, I'd still like to thank you. Here is to you for your part, (which was the hardest), in creating our "one" beautiful and "one" handsome special gift's. I truly thought I would never ever have children. I could have done it with someone else, but the recipe would not have been the same. I am very pleased with our children, especially their personalities. Although we did not make it to that level of honor, which is "marriage", we were still blessed with and very proud to have our two children. I thank you for that. I'd also like to thank you for helping me with keeping my presence felt, even though I am not in the same household as my children. They know without a doubt who's their (daddy), *yes sirrrr!* You know oh so well how I feel about you, the good, and the bad, or at least, what I perceive to be your good and bad behavior. Uh uh uh……. Although you may not want to believe it, I am honored that you are the mother of my children. Peace and Stay blessed!

A special thanks to the Arizona Informant, which has been an ear for our people in Arizona for over thirty-five years.

I would also like to thank the new newspaper, the Write Up. They have different views but they share a common ground, which is us, we the people, the Black/African American community in Arizona.

DEDICATION TO COLUMBIA, MISSOURI

My time in Columbia was a very enlightening phase of my life. I was surrounded by all types of people especially my own Black/African Americans. I can say honestly that Columbia treated me well. All the people at Hickman High School, the people who lived in town and of course the people who lived in Indian Hills accepted me. We were not a bad group of kids. Overall, we were very positive. We put Columbia on the map for breakdancing, head spins, pop locking, ticking, the wave, hip hop, and for having a dance troop The Blind Boone Drill Team. In spite of some negative news, we had people who really cared about us and made sure that we did not get into any trouble. We could not run the streets and if we hung out in the streets we were in front of one of our families' houses. I miss all of you. Columbia gave me some life changing experiences. I still share many great positive memories. May you all stay blessed! Peace!

The Corner Of 224 Lexington, Missouri

What it is, kin folk? Long time no hear. This is the hangout. This was our spot where we could just kick it and unwind. We would share stories about events in our day and our thoughts on life. Everybody, who was everybody, would always bless this spot. Many people who blessed the spot were blood family. Others were people like me, who were embraced and adopted into the family. You see, when you move to the country or are born and raised in the country, this is the treatment you'd receive. For example, if you hear people say, "That is my cousin or (Cuz)," they do not have to be related by blood. This is just country hospitality. We are just showing a person love that is all. May you all be blessed and try to stay strong. I know that this is very difficult at times, especially since; a lot of us have been through and seen many things which have not been so positive. Unfortunately, we have also lost many loved ones; some in a not so good and unexpected way. We mourn, but we must move on. Remember this is a path that we must all take someday. We must also remember an important fact, we will all meet again. When that horn sounds, our spirits will come forth and we will reunite. For the ones who are no longer with us, rest in peace. For the ones of you, who still breathe, enjoy life to the fullest! Take care of your body so that you can live a long full life. Stay blessed! Peace!

ANONYMOUS

I can do this all day. (Thank people, that is.) In saying this, I will state that this is not going to be my only book. This is just the beginning. I am saving that thank you for my up coming entries in history. Therefore, I say this to everyone I have crossed paths with, thank you. Whether it was a good meeting or a bad one, we shared that moment for a reason. That moment affected me somehow and in some way. That is why I thank you as well. As Tupac would say, "I ain't mad at cha." I can honestly say that! I am not mad at anyone anymore. Nevertheless, we learn that people in life are going to "Hate It or Love It!" as in the song by Game, featuring 50 Cent and Mary J. Blige. "Peace and stay blessed."

A SPECIAL DEDICATION TO MY BROTHERS AND SISTERS

Our mother taught us manners and that we should always respect others, although, she never really briefed us on how the world was going to treat us at least, not that I can remember. Was she dreaming that the world would treat us fairly or was it that she just did not want to hurt our feelings? In my opinion, we never really had anyone show us the way to have a successful and promising life. School was not pushed as an important tool for success nor was controlling our credit or being married and raising our children as a strong family. Neither was the emphasis placed toward education brings financial freedom. Nor was the notion that a close family is a strong family as well as a strong family is a close family. I feel the little closeness we do share, we created, which helps us deal with what we are going through in life. Our mother was a single parent and she raised us to the best of her ability. Mom raised us the same way her mother raised her. Grandmother raised Mom the way her mother raised her and so on and so forth. There comes a time when someone has to make a stand and say: "Enough is Enough!" We must break that cycle. It is not a family curse. It is imperative that we stop believing in this. I do not believe in curses. Although, I do believe it is a lack of knowledge. We were all put out early, some even earlier then others. If no one wants to educate us or does not know how to educate us, we must find a way to educate ourselves. We have to make that change and it is never too late. We must stop placing the blame on the past. We must set our focus on the future, in order to live our lives abundantly. Now, for us to live longer we have to be obligated to care for ourselves, with special attention pertaining to our bodies. I love you all the same. We were born from the same mother; therefore, we are the same blood. This is what makes us family. We are and always will be brothers and sisters. Let us keep our families together and strong. The way I see it, it is us against the world. There are seven of us in our family, we can run things if we stick together. Seven is a winning number, therefore, if you mess with one you mess with all. This is necessary for us and it is never too late. I love you all and I want you all to remember that. I also want you to feel comfortable saying, "I LOVE YOU!" Peace. See you soon for our family photo.

My Special Gifts Of Life

My children, I would always talk to you while your mother was carrying you inside her body. I was there for every appointment, even more importantly, I was there the day you inhaled your first breath of air. I would watch you sleep or have you on my shoulders while we both slept. I would like for your journey in this, sometimes not so kind world, to be a much smoother travel then mine has been. I will always love you with all my heart. You should always know that you are indeed my gifts from God! I am very thankful for you. You help me everyday, just by being who you are. I thank you for loving me and respecting me the way you do. Here is something to keep with you throughout your travel. If you ever have a problem staying true to others, always and I do mean always, stay true to yourself and each other. Never allow anyone to disrespect or take advantage of you. Demand respect, and then return respect! You can obtain this by being true to yourself and being yourself. You do not have to hit anyone, Yhamil. Believe me when I say, I know it is hard sometimes but you can handle it. A firm handshake, eye contact, and confidence will suffice. Isis, you know the values Daddy always instills in you, which is, always be a lady, always. That goes for the way you, sit, stand, walk, talk, and carry yourself and your overall presence. This must always be presented. Furthermore, never let any man disrespect you in any form. Nor should you disrespect him but do stand your ground! Handle the situation like the lady you are. Both of you remember, never, ever, do anything to fit in with others. You do not need to be part of any group or organization to be accepted! You only have to please your Heavenly Father and yourself. By chance your inner self provides you with the feeling something is not right; then it is ok to follow that feeling. That insight is a gift and may be your Heavenly Father or your parents up bringing telling you not to do it. If they respect you and or love you, they will never try to harm you. Remember that! Take very good care of one another. You are family! Family is very important! People come and go in our lives, but your family comes in only one set. That set is irreplaceable. Share the knowledge you learn with one another, this is to include your sisters, Allicesa and Simarie. You have four people in your family and you only need to be a part of this group. You hear me? Stay strong my babies and just please remember, to always place God first in your life and you can never go wrong! I love you with all my soul and all my heart!

Your Daddy,

Ryan Edward Strickland

Not About Hate Or Being Militant

My book is not about hate nor is it about being militant. I am not for hate or for being militant. I am, on the other hand, hoping to help create a spark of desire to seek more knowledge toward awareness. Which in return will bring forth the courage to take a stand for something more positive? Furthermore, courage will aid your strength of character to not tolerate anyone who tries to take advantage of you. If someone is willing to hurt you with words or actions, then it is your responsibility to bring him or her to justice. My intent is to help guide you to a more optimistic technique. This in return caters to your stance to remain true to your beliefs which allows you to stand firm against the ones who are trying to bring you down. All I want to do is stimulate your mind. Once stimulated, you can ask yourself, plus others questions, and generate your own concluding factors about life and how it has been and still is treating you today. Even more importantly, it is also about taking responsibility for your actions. However, the main purpose of my book is to raise awareness, and create the spark which will trigger the phenomenon Willie Lynch speaks of so wearily. This phenomenon can bring our people out of the psychological slavery mentality. Once Blacks in America break that bondage, every Black/African American in this world will have achieved unity and true freedom. This broken bondage will bring about new minds that are free of all shackles. Those same shackles which introduced fear, envy, distrust, and disrespect to our race. We will finally have closure. This closure will give us a peaceful mind and much stronger race.

MY INTERPRETATION OF "THA-MAN"

Tha-man is the system which has implemented slavery as being an acceptable lifestyle for human beings.

Tha-man is the invisible hand of slavery.

Tha-man is racism in every form.

Tha-man is whoever is unfair to all humankind.

Tha-man is the one who is against his or her own race.

Tha-man is just like the term nigger, it has no race or gender, but every race and gender has, at one time or another, partaken in its world. We should leave that world behind. It only promotes hatred, segregation, envy, lust, and negativity. Wake up people!

"HOW CAN ANYONE EVEN CONSIDER THEMSELVES AN AMERICAN IF THEY ARE A RACIST? BETTER YET, HOW CAN YOU EVEN BE CONSIDERED HUMANE?"

MY INTERPRETATION OF MY USAGE OF THE TERM "THEY"

"They" is a person who changes stripes, so to speak. "They" have many personalities. "They" are no particular gender. "They" put themselves above you. "They" look down on you and feel you are not worthy to be on their level. "They" are the ones who feel you are not entitled to the same rights as they. "They" do not feel you deserve to breathe the same air they are breathing. "They" are appalled you have the audacity to even think you are entitled to anything they have. "They" tend to use you and discard you when finished. "They" are Bourgeois, self centered, selfish, inconsiderate, ungrateful, self seeking, egotistical users who only see good in themselves and what they are doing, not others. "They" have even considered themselves leaders.

My Use Of The Term "Rise Up"

When America hears a Black/African American man mention the words *"Rise up"* America gets nervous or silent. It is almost like E. F. Hutton is speaking. "When E. F. Hutton speaks, everybody listens." (E. F. Hutton is a financial figure from back in the day.) Please do not be nervous. Just get to know us. Try to understand us. You never had to fear us. That's real! Just so you know, when I reference this term, I am using it as a motivational tool. I'm merely trying to bring more awareness, trust for self and one another, along with harmony, respect, self confidence, responsibility, reliability, to my people in addition to more cooperation amongst my people. This is all, *nothing less*, just more. I do not want anyone harmed or threatened. When I say *my* people, I mean the group or race that I am categorized into by society.

BLACK AMERICANS/AFRICAN AMERICANS

These are my thoughts and views on how we view ourselves. Some of us do not wish to be called African Americans. Some of us do not wish to be called Black Americans. In some cases, this choice is more then just a personal preference. Once we research our history, then and only then will we truly know who we are. In order for us to remember our history we must first know, embrace and preserve our history. Some of us have descendants from Africa and some from England. Others may even have descendants from France and Spain. In fact, some of our descendants were a third race that was never enslaved completely. I say completely because they had some rights. They were a combination of a race: White/Black, Indian/Black, French/Black or Spanish/Black, along with a variety of other mixtures, some even unknown. Still, this did not allow them to share the same rights as whites. This group of somewhat privileged people was called, *"Gen De Couleur Libres"*, or "The Free People of Color." This just goes to show our people are from all parts of the globe.

MY INTERPRETATION OF THE TERM "NIGGER"

I do not like this word. I can truly say that I never have. Have I used it? The answer is rarely, but shamefully, and painfully, yes. My suggestion for this word is, "If we cannot stop using this word for ourselves, let us stop using the word in honor of Richard Pryor." Richard Pryor has influenced many people throughout the world and has gained the respect of most of them. At one time during the 1970's he helped put a halt on the word. We were very proud people and we listened when he said, he himself, was no longer going to utilize the word. In return, many of us took the word out of our own vocabulary. Somewhere along the line we picked this habit up again and infected our race like a plague which has no antidote. Let's put this word to rest for the last time! Deeper then six feet under! Maybe, just maybe, we can't quit cold turkey? If this is the case, allow me to make a suggestion. Please keep in mind that this is merely a suggestion. It may sound crazy at first, but so is the use of that word. My suggestion is to have an "N*****" Out Day, which is very similar to a *"Smoke out Day."* On this day we will not say this word at all. We have given this word too much power. It has affected as well as infected us far too long. After the day ends, we should keep it going for one week. Once we make it through the week, we ought to strive for a whole month. At the end of that month we can set a time at which we should yell this word. We will yell this word as loud as we can one last time in unison. I think that once we really hear how degrading it sounds and how terrible it makes us feel maybe reality will set in. Once reality hits us we will be able to stop using it FOREVER! We can do this in the honor and memory of Richard Pryor.

May he rest in peace.

OR HOW ABOUT THESE

Necro, necrophilia, negro, negroes, negress, negritoid, negritude, negroid, negroidal, negroness, negrophile, negrophilism, negrophilist, negrophobe, negrophobia, niglet, nigra, niggard, niggardly, nigger, niggle, niggling, niggly, the nigger in a woodpile, nigger toe or negrito, nigga, niggas, etc.......

I have not been able to find the exact origin of the word *"nigger"*. However, a friend who is very knowledgeable in the matter informed me that the term *"nigger"* came from the word *Necro*. This is derived from a Greek word which means *to be dead, death, decay,* and *black magic*. It seems to me that everything that is black or deals with being black is portrayed as being bad. Did you know that if you look up the word "nigger" in the dictionary it breaks the term down by gender. "Nigger" is the black man, Negress, is the black woman, and Niglet is the black child. Negro refers to people with dark or black skin who are from Africa. *Negroid* is defined as a black or dark skinned person who has an African Ancestor. This word has many different meanings, and I do mean many. All of which are demeaning to us. For instance, the word "nigger toes." For those of you who have never heard of this term, a "nigger toe" has always been explained to me as a Christmas nut. Reason being, it was only available around this time of the year. Its real name happens to be Brazil nut or Para nut, which is actually a very healthy nut and has a proven history to help with prostate cancer and possibly others. There is also confirmed evidence that the Brazil nut even helps in the early stages of Alzheimer patients. Unfortunately this nut has been referenced as a "nigger toe" for far too many years. The average person does not even know that its real name is Brazil nut. At least not the people who are from my neighborhood! Only in America! Uh, uh, uh…uh As far as I am concerned this rough, ridged, curved, brown, hard shelled nut bears absolutely no resemblance to a Black mans toe or any mans toe. The only way it may even be close, is if the person was a diabetic or had gangrene, and the toe turned colors due to lack of circulation. I commend those of you who are doing your darndest to make this word positive, but to be truthful with you in my opinion; all you are really doing is making it more popular. No matter how we use it or look at it, this word still ends with the same results, negative! This shows in my examples.

I offer this suggestion; instead of putting so much effort in making this

word hip or positive, apply that energy toward something a lot more meaningful, such as unity! That would be cool. Don't you think? Here is something else to think about. We were never considered "niggers" until we were enslaved, which is very similar to the herring. The herring is a fish that is only considered a sardine after it is tightly packed in cans. If you search the ocean, river, lakes or even ponds, you will never find a fish called a sardine. Exactly like the herring stripped of its freedom and renamed after it has been put into captivity, we as Black/African American people were never called or considered "niggers" before we ourselves were stripped of our land, language, culture, freedom then enslaved. Therefore, we need to find out who we are before we accept the names America has instilled on us as humans. Otherwise, we too are adding to the neg, but our suffix has lect at the end. Just in case you do not get it; I will spell it out: N-E-G-L-E-C-T. (Neglect) If we continue to use this word we are neglecting to care for ourselves properly, which also happens to be the definition of the word. Furthermore, we are disrespecting all those whose blood was shed for

our rights up to this point. We should not let America define us, only we should define our-

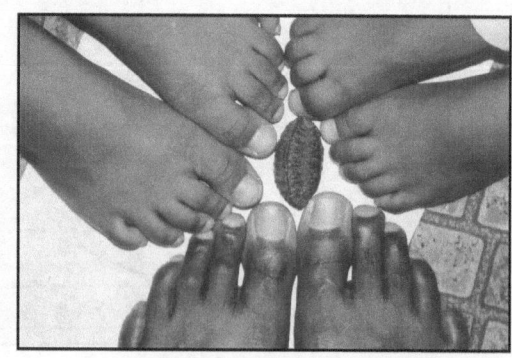

selves! We not only have that power; we are entitled to that right. You know the saying, "If you don't use it, you lose it." Do you want to lose your rights?

If there are still some of you who are not feeling any of the above examples, and they just don't work for you, then how about this one?

This is what we pass down to our sons, and call it stylin; "SAGGIN"! Now let's flip it. This is what we are called; "NIGGAS"! So tell me; how should this be viewed? Should we be viewed as stylin "NIGGAS" or just some "NIGGAS" "SAGGIN?" Does this one work for you? You can still keep your identity when you dress yourself in a more presentable manner.

SHOCKING THE MIND

Good morning, good afternoon, good evening my all-so-faithful, loyal, obedient Niggers, Alligators, Apes, Coons, Possums, Jigger-A-Boos, Moolies, and Spooks. Need I say more? Are you awake yet?

On Tuesday night, November 9, 2004, I read *The Willie Lynch Letter and the Making of a Slave* three times. I am astonished at the self-destructive methods and techniques he used to corrupt the minds of our Black/African American race. This system was put in place with the intent to enslave us for three hundred years or more. At the time however, they never thought twice about this being wrong. All they knew was that they wanted a solution to a problem; a problem which lacked control. Therefore, they required a solution which embodied control. His method is merely one of the first and oldest experiments done on Black/African Americans; which he passed on to other slave owners. He introduced his method of slavery control to the slave owners in Virginia on the banks of the James River in 1712. He boasted how he himself was indeed using this method and how beneficial it had been for him on his own plantation in the West Indies. His whole system is set in place for Black/African American males to fail in his society. His plan is to enslave first the men, then the women, and lastly the children, for hundreds of years. Willie Lynch felt and said that he had a foolproof method for controlling us. Doctors have told us for some time now that psychological abuse is just as bad if not worse than physical abuse.

In his words and I quote, "In my bag here, I have a foolproof method for controlling your black slaves. I guarantee every one of you that if installed correctly, it will control the slaves for at least 300 hundred years. My method is so simple. Any member in the slave owner's family or overseer can use it. I have outlined a number of DIFFERENCES among the slaves and I take these differences and make them BIGGER. I use FEAR, DISTRUST and ENVY for control purposes." They want us to fear them, but God said to fear him only. They want us to distrust and to be envious of each other but to trust and praise them. As Alice Walker once said "No person is your friend who demands your silence or denies your right to grow." We need to rise up as a group now! Stop! Do not accept things the way they are. Realize that each one of us does make a difference in this world. We are not free! Not as free as we should be. I am not asking you to wear out the soles of your Nike's, Lugz, or Stacey Adams; nor am I asking you to sweat up your Ralph Lauren, Tommy Hilfiger, or Versace clothing, by marching, not yet anyways. This is 2008 and we, as Black/African Americans are still invisible until election year. In fact, I am not going to ask anything of you; I am demanding it! I am demanding that we rise up and challenge the system more even when we will not personally benefit from it. We will be more effective in challenging the system when we unite and truly stand united. We must study and learn our Black/African American history. If we do not know what they have done and are still doing to us, then how can we fix it? We need to study them the same way they study us. We must study their history and their system so that we will be more prepared to sit at their table so to speak. For instance, did you know that Timberland, the brand that most of us love so much, may in all probability be owned by the president of the Ku Klux Klan, KKK? If this is true, how is that for supporting the original Lynch mob? History is very important to us. Cheikh Anta Diop once said, "Intellectuals ought to study the past not for the pleasure they find in so doing, but derive lessons from it." Knowledge is much more powerful then brute force, and they know this. They have used knowledge to their advantage for many years. Bruce Lee was a small person, but he was able to beat a lot of people who were much bigger; taller, and stronger; than he. How did he do this you might ask? It is a very simple answer. He outsmarted them. You see, they do not want to see us on their level at all; although, most of us are there. Examples: General Colin Powell; Judge Clarence Thomas, Jesse Jackson; and Bill Cosby, just to name a few.

We as Black/African American men really need to wake the hell up, and smell something besides weed, crack or the crack of someone's ass. We must do a reality check. It's okay to step into the light. We must start performing as a group to make a change in our society.

Tha-Man has, always been and still is, intimidated by us, the Black/African American male. The reason for this is our natural, God-given talents and intelligence. Another reason is our ability to adapt and overcome. Most importantly they are afraid of an uprising by us that will allow us to find a more respectful place in society. It may also be they are threatened by us and feel we may take over and leave them out, or perhaps they are just greedy. We are not out for revenge. We have mentioned reparation, but never revenge or hate. Therefore, if we continue to listen to Tha-Man, follow his directions without doing our own research and never challenging the system in fear of harassment, we will defeat ourselves. This act will leave Tha-Man with a victory over us again. He will have accomplished his mission in keeping us ignorant, isolated and institutionalized in his society. We cannot allow this. I will not allow this. We cannot afford to just bend over and accept what they say to be fact. We have to want the truth and sometimes we have to dig deep to find it. Sometimes the truth is right in our face and we pass it up everyday. This is why, my brothers, we must pay attention to detail, stay alert and be focused.

At times it seems as if the system has institutionalized us, although not all of us are on lockdown. Our ancestors broke free from their physical shackles; we must break free from our mental shackles. Education is the key in accomplishing this. There is an old *African American Folk* saying that goes "If you want to keep something secret from black folks, put it between the covers of a book." This will remain true unless we unite as a group and educate ourselves and each other. Then and only then will we truly overcome. Some of us may have gotten through the system, but until we all succeed in doing so, we have not even put a dent in the system. Let us all come together as one to challenge this system. Pressure by one or two of us will not work! We must come together united before this system will recognize who we are.

Using Our Black Women's Mind Against Us

The Willie Lynch experiment and focus centered on the Black/African American woman. His main reasons for focusing on the woman relate to her ability to nurture. In return she would train her daughter to be independent just like her and not to depend on the Black/African American male. She would also subconsciously train her son to be weak minded and passive not providing any resistance to the system whatsoever. This was said to be her way of protecting him. (Could this be our Mommas' Boy?) However, my focus is first us, the Black/African American males. We are indeed the keys to the lock which will release our race into becoming a more productive and powerful society. We are true natural leaders of the world and Tha-Man knows this. I feel this is one of the main reasons our Black/African American history has been attacked, changed, not taught, or even just left out, of our schools studies. In history they attempted to destroy our STRONG BLACK IMAGE in front of our Black/African American women and children. We must let it be known, in spite of all they have tried to do to us, our IMAGE is still very much present today. We are STRONG and VERY PROUD to be BLACK! Furthermore, there is nothing wrong with this. This is just another form of confidence. We are only saying that we are proud of who we are; and who we are becoming, which is more; POSITIVE and

PRODUCTIVE! The Godfather of Soul, Mr. James Brown said it best, and I quote: "Say it loud, I'm black and I'm proud." Just for the record, no other race has to explain why they are proud to be who they are.

Willie Lynch used the same techniques on us that he used to train and break horses. He put it as follows:

"Now the breaking process is the same for both the horse and uncivilized nigger, use the same processes only slightly vary the degree and step up the pressure so as to do a complete reversal of the mind. Take the meanest and most restless nigger, strip him of his clothes in front of the remaining niggers, the female, and the nigger infant, tar and feather him, tie each leg to a different horse faced in opposite directions, set him a fire and beat both horses to pull him apart in front of the remaining niggers. The next step is to take a bullwhip and beat the remaining nigger male to the point of death in front of the female and the infant. Don't kill him. But put the fear of God in him, for he can be useful for future breeding."

Keep in mind that he wanted us to fear him. If we did so, we would not rise up against him. He wanted to destroy our dignity in front of our women so she would view us as being weak, and view him as being stronger. This was a very important part of his experiment. Willie Lynch tried to strip us of our dignity by publicly humiliating us. He did this in front of our Black/African American women, our children, and the rest of the slave population. Willie Lynch used a much lighter technique on our women. He would test her loyalty and resistance to being obedient. If she failed him in any way, he would not hesitate to punish her. He wrote, "If she shows any signs of resistance in submitting completely to your will, do not hesitate to use the bull whip on her to extract that last bit of bitch out of her. Take care not to kill her, for in doing so, you will spoil good economics. When in complete submission, she will train her offspring in the early years to submit to labor when they become of age. Understanding is the best thing."

PROTECTING YOUR SEED OF ROYALTY

As Black/African American men, society instills in our mind that in order for us to be a manly man, we must be players. We must have many women. We are the MANDINGO. We must (*sow*) SOIL OUR ROYAL OATS. With all of the infectious diseases out there today, that is just what you may end up with, SOILED OATS or better yet, SPOILED OATS. If you have spoiled oats, what good are we to our people? If this takes place, guess what—they win again. Besides, if we have many women, we may have many children. If we have many children then we have to pay many dollars. If we are paying many dollars for our many children then we are working many hours. If we have to work many hours to pay for our many children then we will stay broke and preoccupied for many years. We have to leave the shady sex alone. Sex outside of marriage has done nothing but kept us in debt, one way or another, and helped us fail. We must accept marriage as our way of living. I am tired of hearing so many of us Black/African Americans saying "marriage is not for me." Well, I say, "That's BULL****!" Marriage is acceptable for all the other races so, why should it not be for ours? In fact, they raised their children with the idea that marriage is the most respectable and prosperous way to live. Most of us find shacking up to be more feasible. I know that some of us are practicing marriage but once again, not all of us are. Get married first, before we start our families. Some of us already have children out of wedlock. Do not sweat it, but do learn from it. This is our time to change the way we live. We are in control. Therefore, as they say in the movies, "Cut." "Take two." "Action!" We are now starting over the right way. Do not pass go, but DO STAY OUT OF JAIL! Protect your seed. Protect your seed because it is royalty. We need to control our own race by controlling our seed. The woman who has your children has to be worthy and has to earn that honor. Women are interviewing us and we must interview them. We cannot afford to think about getting "some ass." Get this off of your *brain*. Although some of you have put a new meaning to this word, I am talking about your mind. Do not make any more children unless you are married. There are no exceptions to this law. Yes, I said *LAW*. If this is what it takes to wake you up then consider it so. Contrary to belief, most of us really do not desire to break the law; therefore, this should be a sealed deal. Do you know that if you have one woman and one family you will stay more focused and become a more productive man for many years? Therefore, we should marry, but marry a compatible person; and stay married to this compatible person. We must also practice staying loyal and communicate with our spouse. Furthermore, do your best to treat your spouse the same way you did when you were dating. In other words, whatever you did to get your spouse, do these same things to keep your spouse. Please pay attention to detail. Tha-Man does. This is why he has been able to stay ahead of us for so long. As Black/African American men we have to make a very strong stand to regain first pride in ourselves, then our families, and last but not least, in our people.

Lust Can Be Deceiving

There are many diseases out there and have always been since yesterday, today, and tomorrow. Diseases evolve just like the times we share as the seconds, minutes, hours, days, weeks, months, and years pass us by. Just looking at someone is not going to reveal anything to you. If someone is a carrier or is infected with some disease you will not be able find it in their looks. Imagine if the disease they had revealed itself along their forehead or even across their teeth when they smiled with some sort of highlighted gene. That would be rather nice, wouldn't you agree? Maybe in the future, they will make a mini-portable test for all diseases. Maybe, just maybe, we will ask more questions when we meet a person. Something similar to this:

Ryan: Hello, my name is Ryan Strickland, and yours?

Lady: Shelly Z. Mystery. My friends call me Shelly.

Ryan: Is it ok if I call you Shelly?

Shelly: That is fine.

Ryan: If you do not mind me asking, how old are you?

Shelly: I don't mind. I am 35 and yourself?

Ryan: I am the big 40.

Shelly: Wow, you don't look it. I would have guessed some where in your late 20's early 30's.

Ryan: Thank you. You look rather young yourself, that's why I asked your age.

Ryan: So are you married, divorced, dating or single? When I say single I mean completely single; no strings attached to anyone. I am not looking for any drama, just the chance to get to know a good woman.

Shelly: (Laughs and replies) I understand. I am single, very single.

Ryan: Me too.

Shelly: Any children that you know of?

Ryan: I must proudly say I have two beautiful children, a seven year old son and an eight year old daughter.

Ryan: How about yourself?

Shelly: I have 1. My little man is six.

Shelly: So any baby momma drama?

Ryan: Ha, ha, ha…Nope.

Shelly: How did you manage that?

Ryan: Time to heal I guess.

Ryan: Any diseases?

Shelly: What?

Ryan: Do you have any diseases I should know about?

Shelly: No, I don't think so. What about you?

Ryan: Not that I know of.

Ryan: I did not mean to offend you. It is just so crazy in this day and age. Plus, I'd like to be around to watch my children grow up.

Shelly: Hmmm, you're right. Believe me, I do understand.

Ryan: So Shelly, would you be open to taking this test I have?

Shelly: (Laughing) You're funny. Are you serious?

Ryan: Yes. It's a mini portable testing kit for two. It covers everything from HIV to Herpes and anything in between.

Shelly: Wow, I have never had anyone ask me that before; I am impressed.

Ryan: Thank you, I must say I love all types of women, all shades, all shapes all sizes, but right now I'm really feeling you. You have that natural beauty going on with a hint of Vivica Fox along with a sample of Halle Berry and a pinch of Alicia Keys. Um um ummm. Excuse my slang, but all I can say is....Bangin!

Shelly: (Smiling) Well thank you. You are quite handsome yourself.

Ryan: (Smiles) Thank you.

Sounds funny huh? A mini-portable test….. sounds like a plan to me. In my opinion, we should ask a lot of these questions. I'm not telling you what to do. I am just making a suggestion and giving you something to think about. Peep this. Here is a list of Sexually Transmitted Diseases. Some of them have cures and some do not. When I read about these diseases it made me look at things a lot differently. I must say that when I look at a nice booty, I see the booty first, but then reality sets in. As her booty shakes, and bounces in slow motion as she passes by, my mind starts processing diseases. I ask myself, "Is she good?" "Does she have anything?" "Is she as good as she looks?" Please forgive me. Lord, Lord, Lord….OooooWeeee! I tell you, we are a long way from just getting a shot. That's the luxury our parents had. Times sure have changed and I really view things differently now that I have reviewed this list. I sure hope it does the same for you. Please, do not be afraid to ask questions or to share information with your partner. You can save your life and others. The information comes from all three of the following places:

THE CENTER FOR DISEASE CONTROL CDC:/PLANPARENTHOODANDARIZONA COUNTYHOSPITAL STD'S DEPARTMENT

I am not a doctor. I am just listing these diseases straight from the above sources with comments here and there. I am learning just like you are about these types of diseases. Some of them I had no idea existed. Some I can't even pronounce. So please do further research on your own for your own benefit. Do not just take my word for it by all means. Please do your own research and find your own answers to your questions. Most of these diseases are transmitted with any form of sexually activity. USE YOUR IMAGINATION. All symptoms varies with disease some diseases may not show any symptoms at all. You can have a disease or be a carrier for years and not even know it. So please educate yourself, protect yourself or sustain until you are really ready to deal with the sexual experience. It may not lead you to a good experience. I am sure there are plenty of first timers who can attest to that.

SYPHILIS: Shows no symptoms but **curable in early stages**. No real age limit, Babies to Adults. You can carry this disease for years and not know.

BACTERIAL VAGINOSIS BV: Symptoms: Discharge, order, pain, itch, burning. **Curable** but must be treated to prevent or complications. 16% of pregnant women have this. Scientist, are still unsure on how to prevent this.

CHLAMYDIA & LYMPHOGRANULOMA VERNEREUM LGV: No symptoms for women. Symptoms for men are discharge from penis. **Curable**

but can cause problems especially for women's reproductive system if not detected early.

GONORRHEA: symptoms: **Curable now**, but different types are occurring. Most women will have no symptoms and if so they will be mild. Many men may or may not display any symptoms. Also the time frame may vary from two to five days or as long as thirty. A burning sensation while trying to use the bathroom; along with a white, yellow or green discharge may be present. This disease is very high in the Black/African American community, especially among the teenagers to adults.

HEPATITIS (VIRAL) HBV: HEPATITIS B NO CURE, SHOWS NO SIGNS! THIS IS A VERY SERIOUS LIVER DISEASE. AFFECTS ALL AGES, AS MANY AS 1 OUT OF 20 CAN HAVE IT AND AS MANY AS 5000 WILL DIE FROM THE SICKNESS CAUSED BY HBV. YOU CAN SPREAD IT AND NEVER KNOW IT. THERE ARE **FIVE** TYPES OF HEPATITIS RANGES: **A, B, C, D, AND E.**

HUMAN PAPILLOMA VIRUS INFECTION HPV: symptoms: MAY DISPLAY WARTS IN GENTIAL AREA AND SOME MEN MAY HAVE ABDOMINAL PAIN. **NO CURE** BUT THERE IS TREATMENT. THERE ARE 100 DIFFERENT STRAINS OR TYPES. THERE IS A RANGE YOU MAY FALL UNDER WHICH IS: 6-11 LOW RISK AND 16-18 HIGHEST. THIS DOES AFFECT BOTH MEN AND WOMEN.

(The men and young boys can be carriers and pass this disease on to your daughters. You can request a shot to help protect your daughters from this disease before they get it. Gardasil is the shot they give to young girls ages 9-26 and older. If you have warts, they a cream called Aldara which is used for both men and women. The cream works with your ammine system, but you still have to seek treatment.

HERPES (TWO TYPES 1 & 2) SYMPTOMS: MAY OR MAY NOT BE DISPLAYED. HERPES TYPE 1 IS ABOVE THE WAIST AND TYPE 2 IS BELOW THE WAIST. **NO CURE**. IF YOU DO SHOW ANY SYMPTOMS, IT MAY COME IN THE FORM OF GENTIAL WARTS, WHICH IS TYPE 2. THE OTHER SYMPTOMS MY COME IN THE FORM OF COLD SORES WHICH MAY APPEAR AROUND THE MOUTH, WHICH IS TYPE 1. HOWEVER, YOU CAN PASS HERPES TYPE 1 DURING SEX BELOW THE WAIST; WHICH WILL GIVE YOUR PARTNER GENTIAL HERPES. Herpes can be self transmitted. 1 in 5 Adults have herpes, but of those inflicted are unaware of it, due to the symptoms or lack of symptoms. 50 Million Cases are currently estimated to exist in either active or dormant stages. 1 0f 6 Members of the general infected population is thought to shed active virus occasionally without symptoms. The statistics are there to grab the attention of the public so you can be more conscious of how these diseases can affect your life. The symptoms are mild to none and can go years undetected. You can receive a test without showing symptoms. The test is conducted through a blood sample.

PELVIC INFLAMMATORY DISEASE PID: CURABLE, SYMPTOMS ARE VERY MILD AND CAN GO UNDETECTED. YOU MAY OR MAY DISPLAY PAIN OR DISCHARGE. ALTHOUGH THE DISCHARGE MY BE DUE TO ANOTHER DISEASE LIKE, CHLAMYDIA OR GONORRHEA THIS CAN CAUSE MAJOR PROBLEMS IN YOUNG WOMEN 25 AND UNDER. 100,000 WOMEN IN THIS AGE BRACKET BECOME INFERTILE DUE TO THIS DISEASE EACH YEAR.

TRICHOMONIASIS: Symptoms In women are signs of frothy, yellow, green vaginal discharge with a strong odor. Symptoms in Men may temporarily have an irritation inside the penis, mild discharge, or slight burning after urination or ejaculation. This is a common curable disease in both young men and women. The reason this disease is different is from reversal of detection. The women show the symptoms and the men rarely do. 7.4 Million Cases occur each in young women and men. Men can only get this from women. However women can pass it to another woman.

HIV/AIDS: NON CURABLE AS FAR AS WE KNOW. IT IS VERY CAPABLE OF BE-ING PASSED WITH ANY OF THE ABOVE STD'S. THEY HAVE TREATMENT TO HELP YOUR BODY DEAL WITH THE DIS-EASE. HOWEVER, IT CAN AID IN THE CAUSE OF DEATH DUE TO COMPLICA-TIONS OF SOME OTHER ILLNESS WHICH MAY HAVE BEEN CURABLE.

Please take proper precautions. Your life and the life of others depend on your decision. This is just the tip of the iceberg people. We really need to be more responsible and aware of things and must take better care of ourselves. Another thing, I highly recommend everyone get tested. STD information and referrals to STD Clinics CDC-INFO 1-800-CDC-INFO (800-232-4636) TTY: 1-888-232-6348 In English, en Espanola National Herpes Hot-line (919) 361-8488

CONTAMINATION IS DOMINATION

Another problem my brother, is the drug and alcohol usage. This is merely another distraction. It has put us in a disillusioned world for far too long. Most of us would rather stay in that world because then we don't have to face reality. Hell, in that state of mind, we are equal. We figure if we stay in that world we are on top of the world, but all the while in the real world, we are being ridiculed. Once we wake up and stop hiding behind a fake-ass wall, we will be able to face our fears and this system, which Tha-Man so kindly set in place for us. We most definitely will be a strong force to be reckoned with. Here is an example of the easy way out. We all know that drugs were brought into our community. Have you ever thought about how the average Black/African American teenager attained his skills on converting powdered cocaine into the rock form? Which, on the street is notoriously known as **crack**? It might be me, but unless I was absent that day in Chemistry class, I really do not recall Crack 101 being a requirement to graduate! Instead of rejecting the drugs, we embraced them. We even went as far as making a living off of them as if it was an honest job. Never mind what it is doing to our people; *I am gettin paid*. Once again, it might be me, but are we stupid, greedy or both? Come on now, we have to realize that the whole thing was a setup from the get go. Well I guess not, since some of us even went as far as selling to our mothers, fathers,

sisters, brothers, aunts, uncles, and cousins, all in the
name of the almighty dollar. We just said, to hell with
our morals and threw them out the damn door. Little
did we know that Tha-Man was counting on that! He
was hoping that we would get our people hooked on
the drug. However, he got an even better deal, since
we, ourselves, would also get hooked on that *paper*
(Money). Did you catch that? Our people Addicted
(hooked) on the drug and we the Dealer Addicted
(hooked) to the *money* or the *flow* of it! We did not
even stop to think that the clientele we felt were so loyal
were our peeps. **Our peeps. (Meaning: our people
of The Black/African American Community.) Our
peeps** would be so lucky, if we were as loyal to them,
as we are to Tha-Man, and they are to us. Though,
I will give us some credit being that we did indeed
stay loyal to Tha-Man, but did Tha-Man stay loyal
to us? HELL NAW! Especially, when he thought
we had become too much of a "Big Shot Baller." So
Tha-Man slams the hammer down on us and sends
us to tha pen. **Tha pen,** Tha-Mans' Multi-Billion-
Dollar Establishment; and is now the home to many
Black/African American Entrepreneurs. Please pay
attention to detail. Here is something else to think
about. As soon as the neighborhood drug dealer is
busted, another man is quick to pick up the torch and
take his place even though he knows what his fate may
be. On the other hand, when we have positive role
models who are fighting for our rights to be equal and
he or she gets too big and rubs someone the wrong

way, that role model gets MURRR-DERED (e.g., Medgar Evers; Dr. Martin Luther King Jr., Malcolm X; and many other civil rights leaders). No one, I mean no one, is as quick to pick up this torch. There have been and still are many Black/African Americans making many accomplishments and I am not taking or trying to take anything away from any of them. Sometimes we lose track of our main goals, but now we must get back to the basics. We must reach the level of the late Dr. Martin Luther King Jr. and then surpass it. He should be considered a mentor and we his students. It should be our goal and responsibility to try to achieve a higher level of greatness. This is what all great mentors want from their students. This is a sign of respect. On the other hand it should also be considered disrespectful, disobedient and disappointing if we do not reach a higher level of growth. We cannot afford to go through the motions. If we do not reach this growth, we will deliver to the Tha-Man another victorious victory over us. Why is this? Is it Fear? I spit on fear. So shall we all once we unite. Dr. Martin Luther King Jr. once said, "A man who won't die for something is not fit to live."

THANKS FROM THA-MAN

Tha-Man makes light of us in our everyday struggles to survive in this system. They thank us with a sarcastic tone. They praise us for not having unity amongst our race. They praise us for not having our own businesses. They thank us for not supporting those of us who have a business. They thank us for killing each other and not embracing our society. They thank us for fighting their battles. They thank us for all these things even though they still consider us three-fifths of a man. They thank us for not being educated. They thank us for the labor we do leaving time for them to be the businesspeople. They thank us for treating our women badly and disrespecting them. They thank our women for treating us badly and for resisting our beliefs and accepting theirs. They thank us for allowing them to be with our women, but they despise us for being with their women. In this day and age, we may hear people speaking about how Black/African Men are always after White/Caucasian Women. This may or may not be true, but the fact of the matter is that when there were slaves in America and other places, the White/Caucasian Men always fancied the Women of color. They went as far as organizing a ball called Placage, and if any children were conceived from this union, they would be caught up between the two worlds. Therefore I ask you, who has been doing this longer? White/Caucasian Women have always admired the Black/African Man.

Although it was very acceptable for White/Caucasian Men to be with a Woman of Color, it was considered a disgrace for White/Caucasian Women to be with a Man of Color. If she was caught having sex with a Black/African Slave, it was very possible she would yell rape. If she was not caught in the direct sexual act, but conceived a child from her willing and sometimes *seductive union*, she and her *child* would be allowed to **bleed to death**. This was a very immoral act, but it was indeed the punishment for this so-called crime. In the present day, if they show an interracial couple in: *soaps*, *sitcoms*, and *movies*, it just so happens to be a White/Caucasian Man with a Black/African American Woman. Now they have shown on rare occasions a Black/African American man with a White/Caucasian woman, but just on rare occasions. That's all I'm saying, that's .....All...I'm saying. Is anything wrong with this? Is anything right with this? I, myself, ask this question. Maybe you should ask yourself? Either way it is something to think about.

Here is something else they thank us for. They thank us for not controlling our finances. Therefore, I offer this example of a budget as a guide.

A Household Or Christian Budget

God does not want us to be broke. He would like us to be great and to have great things. God does not require equal giving; God requires equal sacrifice. Therefore, we must create a budget. With a budget, we can control our cash flow. This, in return, will allow us to improve our lifestyle and improve our credit. You have at least thirty days to pay a bill before it is reported to the three nationwide credit bureaus (Equifax, Experian, and Transunion.) You can get one free credit report per year by calling this number: 1-877-322-8228. Some creditors will run your credit before they give you service, but they will not report your activities unless you go into default. With this in mind, I recommend the following: if possible, put down a deposit with these types of creditors; it will save you an *inquiry* on your credit report. Although they tell you it will not affect your score, each *inquiry* will affect your score; especially when your credit report shows a lot of *inquiries*. Now let us really get down to business and discuss making a budget for ourselves. Here is an example of a budget. ***Use this as a guide to create a budget that fits your lifestyle.*** Always try to keep a positive account balance. Even if your balance is zero, this is still positive. This is based on a monthly income of $3,333.33 a month, and is $1,666.67 every two weeks and $833.33 every week. Let's say that December's bills are all paid. Your paycheck on December, 2007 is for the first two weeks of January,

2008. Below is a list of creditors for the month. Keep in mind that these creditors may differ per individual and that rates may vary slightly. However, they will remain the same for the most part. With this chart, your monthly total is $2,674.91 and you are working with an income of $3,333.33 a month.

1) Rent: $550.00

2) Car: $330.00

3) Insurance: $142.00

4) Child Support: $444.00

5) Water: $25.00/ Waste: $48.00

6) Gas: $50.00

7) Monthly Tithes: $333.33

8) Weekly Tithes: $83.34

9) Cable: $68.84

10) Home Phone: $89.90

11) Groceries: $300.00

12) Utilities: $85.00

13) Transportation: $140.00

14) Cell: $68.84

15) Biweekly Tithes: $166.67

The Decembers, paycheck covers rent, the car payment, and tithes, which total $1,046.67. This leaves you $620.00, and out of this amount, you have to buy $150.00 worth of groceries and set aside $70.00

for gas to get you through until your next payday. Now you have a remaining balance of $400.00. With some of this, you can knock out some of your smaller expenses, such as gas ($50.00) and cell phone charges ($68.84.) Here is your new balance: $281.16. This is bankable, and it is for emergency use only. If no emergencies come about, it should be added to your next payday balance of $1,666.67, which falls on January, 2008. Now your new total is $1,947.83. With this check, you are to pay the remaining of your monthly bills, which total $1,146.41. After these bills are paid, your new balance is $801.42. Your next payday is January, 2008, remember, this check is for the first part of February and your account is looking good. This check brings your balance to $2,468.09. This puts you ahead and in charge of your bills instead of your bills being in charge of you. This is how it is supposed to be. Remember, God has great credit and the best layaway plan, so who needs Wal-Mart? Ha ha. Stay focused! Just because you have a few extra dollars in your account, do not let it burn holes in your pockets. If you stay focused and well disciplined (and it is going to take much discipline), you can have at a minimal a total of $281.16 extra per month. This total is $3373.92 a year. How is that for a bonus? This is not impossible and it is easy to accomplish if you keep your faith and put God first. Also, eliminate negative thoughts, negative people, and most importantly, stay true to yourself. Now last, but surely not least, truly stay in control of your money and do not let your money control you. May you all continue to stay blessed! This budget is based on a salary of $40,000.00 a year, before taxes paid biweekly. We know that *all people's income varies* and that *emergencies* occur; this is just a *guideline* put together with our people's interest in mind. It is time that we make changes for a better lifestyle. A better lifestyle is the lifestyle that God intended us to live. Another great piece of information is this: Did you know that you are allowed to pay your everyday household bills (*Gas, Lights, Phone, and Groceries*) with your credit cards? You are allowed to pay any bill you have that has not been financed. If you do this, it is as if you are paying yourself. The reason for this is you will beat the interest rate you are paying for your credit card. If you have one or more, use them wisely. Do not pay the credit card companies for giving you the credit card! That is something you earned, and that is your reward. Flip the script. When you use your credit card wisely, it is as if they are paying you for advertising for their company. Think about that. "Good looking out, Anthony!"

Here are the phone numbers and web addresses of all three credit bureaus:

EXPERIAN – XPN	EQUIFAX - EFX	TRANS-UNION
1-888-397-3742	1-800-685-1111	– TU
www.experian.com	www.equifax.com	1-800-916-8800
		(8:30-4:30 M/F)
		www.transunion.com

All three credit reports with credit scores cost $45.00. Your three credit reports alone cost $32.00. But keep in mind that you can get a copy of your credit report free every year or anytime you have been turned down for credit. Here is a toll-free number and address: 1-800-576-2990 (if local, call 602-744-3774).

Corporate Office (open 8:00 a.m. to 5:00 p.m. Monday–Friday Mountain time)

Merchants Information Solution

301 E. Virginia, 2nd Floor

Phoenix, AZ 85004

Now to cover some of the other things we are recognized for. They thank us, and I quote, for not listening to "African American leaders like: Washington, Delaney, Garvey, Bethune, Tubman, and Truth." These are souls who were willing to make a stand for equal justice for our people and who were willing to die for the cause if need be. They fought to bring unity and awareness to us all. They were labeled and viewed as Rebels just because they wanted us to be seen and treated as EQUALS and as HUMAN BEINGS.

They thank us for not fighting for the 13th, 14th, and 15th Amendments, which were written for us Black/African Americans, but are now shared by many. (The 13th Amendment deals with the Abolition of Slavery, and the 14th Amendment deals with our Civil Rights. The 15th Amendment deals with Black Suffrage. It pertains to our rights as Citizens by allowing us the right to vote.) There is a (GRANDFATHER CLAUSE) to the 15th Amendment set in place to deny us our right to vote, which was declared unconstitutional in 1915 and 1939. This amendment was proposed on June 13, 1866 and ratified on July 9, 1868. Did you know that in 2007, our "VOTING RIGHTS" EXPIRE? "WHAT THA!!!!" I had to write the President about this. I vote and I am a concerned citizen. All I can do is ask and make a suggestion. What is the saying: A closed mouth doesn't get fed. I am not ashamed to say in this case that, I'm hungry.

My Letter To The President

Honorable George W. Bush,

I am writing you this letter with the concern of our country in mind. I am a soldier who is now a disabled veteran. I served our country for a total of eighteen years and received an honorable discharge. Although this letter is not solely about me, this letter is about all of us as United States Citizens.

Our Founding Fathers wrote the Amendments with opportunity to excel with the times. The 15th Amendment is my main interest. If I may, I would like to offer you, the Senate, and the House of Representatives of the United States of American Congress this suggestion. Instead of renewing the right to vote for Black/African American Citizens, abolish it or retire it with the slave act. We are all Americans, thus should it not reflect as such? Therefore, is it possible to add a new Amendment or Law that states that all American citizens are entitled to this right? With this in place we will never have to have an Amendment or Law to be signed by another president again after you? This will truly send a very strong statement that times have changed and that we, as Black/African Americans, are with no doubt recognized in history as Citizens of the United States of America.

This will be a win-win situation for us all. All of the citizens of the United States of America; who also have made sacrifices to make this country a truly equal opportunity country. As well as you, sir, Commander in Chief, Honorable George W. Bush, President of the United States of America, will stand firm with other Presidents before you who led this nation in an unforgettable legacy. Will you please accept my suggestion with the utmost respect? It is without question in your power to rewrite history as we know it. May God continue to guide you in your decision making and bless you and your family!

Response Requested

Thank you sincerely,

Ryan E. Strickland

I's Ain't No Nigger An's U's No Nigger Neither

The other thing they thank us for is the most important factor of all my brothers. This is simple, but it is still quite a difficult feat to be accomplished by us as Black/African Americans. The Queen of Soul sang it in one of her hit songs. In fact, she spelled it out. Does any know what that is? R.E.S.P.E.C.T., which I say means this: "Respect Everybody Stand Proud Every brother Come Together." They thank us for not respecting one another. This means that we must let go of all of the derogatory names we have for our race. Such as: bitch, ho, slut, hoochie, chicken head, scrub, and especially nigger, nigga, and negro, just to name a few, since we all know I can be here all day, but I have a point to make. Exhale my brothers. Let go. Letting go of these words is not going to kill us. We have been through worse. Letting go of these negative words will most definitely make us stronger. Tupac tried to turn a negative into a positive by saying N.I.G.G.A. meant: "Never Ignorant Getting Goals Accomplished." Although this was a very worthy effort, to be honest, no matter how we look at it, it is, it has been, and it always will be a negative for our race. Richard Pryor once said he'd always use to use the word nigger when he talked to his audience. He said, one morning he woke up and vowed to never use that word again. Why? People asked. He replied, "Because there are none out there." This had a major impact on our race for a long while, and we were proud to be Black/African Americans. Somewhere along the way, we got sidetracked and lost vision of our goals in our fight for unity and freedom. We settled out of court with no fee and no freedom. I am tired of being called a nigger. Are you tired of being called a nigger? Are you going out like that? I ask you again, ARE YOU GOING OUT LIKE THAT? If we were in the hood, none of us would go out like that. We are all so quick to speak out against, beat down, or even kill our own. Nevertheless, we are very hesitant to step out against "Tha-Man. Hear this: he is only that—a man. They are all only men who can be easily defeated with unity. Queen Latifah sang this one. "U-N-I-T-Y." If you are truly tired of being called a nigger, prove it. Stop using that awful word that was used toward our ancestors to degrade them, saying they were lesser humans. We, as Black/African American men must realize, no matter what our last names are, no matter how educated or rich we may become; we are all only as strong as the less fortunate in our race. We all reflect one another, no matter how good or bad we may be, like it or not. We only reflect one another, not to be mistaken with being accountable for one another. The bottom line is, if we do not respect ourselves, then how can we demand and expect anyone else to? Does this make sense? Vernon Reid once said, "In Africa, there are no niggers; and I will die before I become a nigger for your entertainment."

Boo Nigga Boo

Boo Nigga Boo are you afraid of your own shadow
Boo Nigga Boo do you let people use you
Boo, Nigga Boo do you let discrimination go
unanswered
Boo Nigga Boo do you blame the system for your
mistakes and failures
Boo Nigga Boo do you not take responsibility for your
own action
Boo Nigga Boo do you degrade yourself or your race
Boo Nigga Boo do you call yourself a Nigga
Boo Nigga Boo do you think that you will never make
it in this world
Boo Nigga Boo do you think that your failure is due to
a curse that was placed upon your family
Boo Nigga Boo do you know where you are
Boo Nigga Boo
You can't be asleep, especially if you look like me
Therefore, I cannot say "Wake up, Nigga"
Cause In my dreams, ain't no "Nigger" or a "Nigga"
So where U B
Do subconscious memories of Ancestral Slavery
enslave you?
Even they tried to escape the shackles they bear
Around their necks, wrists, and ankles
Boo, do not be scurrd
Boo, do not be fooled
Boo
There are no "Niggers" or "Niggas" out there

Isn't that cool
So let us escape the Mental Shackles we bear
Because there is a better life out there
Did you hear?
There is a better life out there

Now from this I am saying, the "Nigger" is not a person, but a state of mind; a state of mind of ignorance. Knowledge will free the "nigger" state of mind! In Africa the Black man was intelligent; he spoke, read and understood the language. When the Black man was brought to an unfamiliar surrounding, which brought forth a new language, new system and new laws; this is what the Black man's ignorant to. The Black man was, is and will always be intelligent, but we are all ignorant to what we don't know. This is why knowledge is so important. This is why Master P feels it is so important to send his son to college. Now isn't that cool?

James Baldwin once said, "You can only be destroyed by believing that you're really what the White World calls a Nigger." Now, I ask you all this, by us using this word against ourselves, does this mean we believe that we are "Niggers?" Hmmm...?

NEVER FEEL BAD FOR DOING WHAT'S RIGHT

We should ask ourselves why people try to make us feel bad when we recognize discrimination. The first thing they say is that we are pulling the race card. My questions are: who invented this race card game and how is it played? What is the race card? What does it look like? Has anyone ever seen this invisible, degrading, so called magical device? Who holds this item? Is this an issued item such as food stamps or some other government assistants? I also like to add that the people or person who invented the race card has clearly never been on the receiving end of racism. Otherwise they would not hold their less sensitive attitude towards this plague. Given that they pick cards as an analogy of this ruthless game of theirs, let's play spades, shall we? If they want to call us out saying that we are pulling the so called *Race card.* Then we should call them out on **Discrimination** and pull from their deck of Discrimination until every card in their deck of Discrimination is gone. If we do this every single time, then eventually, they will not be so quick to discriminate against us. Look, this is only an illustration nothing more then that. While we are making our way through life why not make a *Strong Stance.* Let us take this life as if we are playing a game of spades. If we partner up then we will be *"trump tight"*. Therefore, we will be able to run a Boston on their asses! You feel me? Why should we feel guilty for something they are doing to us? We are not at fault, they are! Tha-man and his system have repressed us for far too many years. The sad thing is we have allowed it. Let us play the game of life in a more positive and wise manner. It is our time to show the world that we are not looking for handouts. We have always contributed plus still contribute to this country in a positive way. We do count. We are not the stereotypical, dope users, drug dealers, deadbeat dads or moms, welfare cases, inmates, child support cases, or commodity-cheese eaters.

Finally, my brother, observe every angle. We can no longer afford to point fingers. We must instead take responsibility for our own actions too. Find solutions. As well as seek God. This does not have to be a vicious cycle. Unite. In 1901, Booker T. Washington stated, "The individual who can do something that the world wants done will, in the end, make his way regardless of his race."

According to recent studies and "The Write-Up" Black/African Americans spent $845 Billion Dollars in 2007. With this in mind my personal opinion is we should really reconsider a **take two** on the NATIONAL BLACKOUT DAY? NATIONAL BLACKOUT DAY is a single day which is selected by the Black/African American community. We would decide on the day and month to boycott the spending of our hard earned money. It is a great idea; and a perfect example of our worth if done properly. The day and idea was created by www.ColorOfChange.org We should allow the facts and numbers to speak for us. We should not be afraid to make or take a stance for something positive. We all know that some of us Black/African Americans have made a stance for things of lesser value. So let us do something positive together and do it for a purpose that really counts.

GROOMING FOOLS

We need knowledge! Willie Lynch said, and I quote:

"You take a slave, if you teach him all about your language, he will know all you secrets, and he is then no more a slave, for you can't fool him any longer, and BEING A FOOL IS ONE OF THE BASIC INGREDIENTS OF AND INCIDENTS TO THE MAINTENANCE OF THE SLAVERY SYSTEM. For example if you told a slave that he must perform in getting 'OUR CROPS' and he knows the language well, he would know that 'OUR CROPS' didn't mean 'OUR CROPS,' and the slavery system would break down, for he would relate on the basis of what 'OUR CROPS' really meant. So you have to be careful in setting up the new language for the slave would soon be in your house, talking to you as 'MAN TO MAN' and that is death to our economic system."

In other words, if we had known the system, we probably would have responded by saying, "Stop playing. Those are not my crops. Those crops belong to you, boss." That would have been the end of the slave mindset, or even one better, that slave! Hmmm. Willie Lynch invented his system to keep our people stupid, scared, and in the shadows of first, "Tha-Man", second society, and third our Black/African American women. It is indeed a well-thought-out and scientific psychological experiment that has hindered our people for far too long. Now it is time for us to flip the script. VETO IT. IT IS A NO-GO at this station. This is our time. It is our time as Americans to rise to a complete new level of living. Our ethnic background should no longer be a factor or an excuse to our existence or to our success any longer.

CHRIS ROCK once said: "A Black Man Is Born a Suspect!"

With this said can you imagine this: A single black mother is being rushed to the hospital. They get her to the delivery room. She is prepared. The doctor starts the delivery. The doctor announces I see the head. Push, you're almost finished. Breathe, one more push. Yes, yes, yes, it's a baby boy. They clean up the baby and hand him to his mother.

The doctor leaves the room. She returns with the police. The police request that the mother turn over her newborn son. She asked you want my son? Where are you taking him? The police pull out some miniature handcuffs, ankle cuffs plus a belly chain. He places them on the baby. The mother starts crying and yelling, stop! Don't do that to my baby! Please do not take my baby. He's just a baby he hasn't done anything. The police replies, yes he has. He has committed his first crime; he was born. I'm taking him into custody before he commits anymore crimes. The mother is screaming noooo. Noooooooo….. Give me back my baby!

This sounds ridiculous and maybe even foolish, huh?

Montel had aired an episode in late 2006 or early 2007, which pertains to black people, somewhere down south, who were deprived the right to bear children. The government assumed the black race was irresponsible and incapable of handling this God given honor. Not only did this have an effect on the black women, but it also involved the black men. The government felt deemed it was responsible to do something in order to control the crime rate from its continuous rise. Their solution was stopping the reproduction of the black race. They did a medical procedure which they neutered and in some cases even butchered the black men and women's reproduction organs so they could never reproduce. This procedure was and is irreversible. This was their answer. This heartless act was their answer to preventing crime in their state and the world. This is beyond words and hate, even more so, it is cruel and inhumane. Furthermore, it was intentionally made irreversible, which meant they were really trying to rid the world of the black race completely. I presume people missed this, which has magnificent, significance. The Black Americans afflicted with this long-term affect of mental and physical torture, have been unable to sue for this act of prejudice.

Now, does the above analogy still appear to be impractical or extreme? Well, if we do not stop and pay attention to things, this could become reality. We, as black people, have been a part of an injustice for many years. More then history has even recorded or cared to record for our history books. You can complain or you can make a change. You can drink and do drugs to try to forget about these types of injustices among others. Better yet you can clean yourself up and stay alert. You can run around and act like this does not affect you when it does. On the other hand you can admit to yourself it does bother you and take action. We all have choices. We just have to make or try to make the right choices. Our life of existence as Black/African Americans depends on us educating ourselves. One other truth toward our continuation also depends upon us uniting instead of separating.

RISE UP

Rise up, my Brother; let us make a stand against the invisible hand. RIse up, my Brother; let us make a stand against Tha-Man. RISe up, my Brother; let us make a challenge against the system. RISE up, my Brother; let us make a stand for the land that our people died for. RISE Up, my Brother; let us raise our voices loud, loud enough to be heard so that our faces can finally be seen. RISE UP MY BROTHER, let us raise our confidence level. Marcus Garvey once said, "If you have no confidence in self you are twice defeated in the race of life. With confidence you have won even before you have started." RISE UP MY BROTHER; LET US MAKE A STAND FOR THE UNITY OF OUR RACE. Society will have no choice but to respect us and view us in a more productive manner. We must pay attention to detail; Tha-Man does. That is why he has been able to stay ahead of us for so long. RISE UP MY BROTHER.

We, as Black/African American men, have to make a very strong stand to regain our pride in firstly ourselves, secondly our families, and then our people. Once all of us gain more knowledge and learn their system, just being a part of it will automatically alter it. This way we can take our rightful place out front as proud, Black/African American men being the heads of our houses and leading our families. We will see eye to eye. We will be on their level; destroying their economic system and creating a new and improved system in which all men are truly viewed equally. Muhammad Ali once said, "If you give people who lived in the slums 93 million dollars, it will be a slum again in twenty-four hours; but if you educate them and then give those same people 93 million dollars the slum can become a paradise." Willie Lynch did not want our people to be viewed as equals, especially the Black/African American male. God has a different plan for us; and he created us all as equals.

We, as the Black/African American race, have never intentionally harmed anyone. We have, however, been forced to defend ourselves. Just because you hear the words *rise up* does not mean that we are militant. This has nothing to do with being militant. This is not about hate. This is about us as the Black/African American man being viewed as a **man** and not being repressed. We must achieve and receive a more positive image, and not the image of a stereotype. Our main goal in this journey is to get what is rightfully ours. We are demanding our voices to be heard as equal participants in the decision making of our country. Our country; the place we help to shape, mold, and build. We have already earned that right with many years of ancestral bloodshed. It is about time; don't you think? We are truly tired of being a shadow, crossing over, or kissing up to hold jobs. We are especially tired of all of the mind games that are played against us. Ok now listen to this:

Is it all about us fitting into the way they want us to be viewed? They want it, so we have to do it. I know some people who have done this one. Did you know that some of us Black/African American change our name or our children's name just to fit in or to get a job? Is this right? Is it? Since when is it right for me to change my name or my children's name just so we can fit in or to get a job? Well I say this is not right. I say so to say this: chances are when we show up and once they see who we are, and our names do not fit our race; we won't get the job or position anyway. This has been a personal experience for me. Furthermore, it has happened quite a few times. Needless to say some of those experiences, I was in the Military. So if we do this, are we saying that we as Black/African Americans should have two names on our birth certificates? How would that look? Let's see, Hmmm... one name for home and one name to fit into society? So I should tell my daughter I named her Shaniquya, but when we are in public her street name is Stephanie? Should I tell my son that I named him Talibe, but in public his name is Tony? I am not; nor did I do this nonsense! On the other hand, what I will do and am trying to instill in my children is this; I tell them to wear their names with confidence and pride. I also told them to allow their actions and credentials to speak for themselves. I place strong beliefs in them towards getting their degrees and pursue being business owners. I just feel this will be a better option and will prove to be more favorable. We are here and we are never leaving. Therefore you can like it or not. If you do not like it, you might as well get used to it. We are staying!

LETTERS WRITTEN BY ME THAT WERE PUT ON THE INTERNET AND IN THE NEWSPAPER

Strickland

Age: 39

Subject: Black People and The Nigger?

Hello Steve, My name is Ryan Edward Strickland. I want to say that we, as Black People, should stop and ask ourselves whether we want to be respected. If our answer is yes, then we need to stop degrading ourselves. I like the movie *White Chicks*, but they used the word and everyone laughed. Richard Pryor quit using that degrading word a long time ago after he and Isaac Hayes visited Africa. Paul Mooney walked with Richard Pryor on his TV show while they were walking their way into history. He should have stopped using the word along time ago. I feel that we should never use anything that has been put in place to degrade us. We, as Black People, tend to always turn bad things into good things. Even the word *bad* means *good* to us. Although it is a good effort, we really need to leave the "N" alone, because all it is causing our race is neg-glect. We must put an end to it before anyone else will. On the other hand, if they want to call us out on saying that, we are pulling the race card. Then we should call them out on discrimination and pull from their deck of discrimination until every card in their deck of discrimination is gone. If we do this every time, then they will eventually not be so quick to discriminate against us.

I ask you all again, Is Your Mind Shackle Free? Our ancestors broke the physical shackles, and we will break the psychological shackles. If we come together and stand strong, we can create that *whirlwind phenomenon* that Willie Lynch spoke of and break the cycle of the First true black-on-black crime. Most of us black people have always put God first, but God truly helps those who help themselves. We can pray all day long, but we must also take action! If it ain't broke—and I do mean ain't—then do not fix it. Rev. Dr. Martin Luther King Jr. and Rev. Jesse Jackson and many others marched and boycotted in the past to get things done and it worked, so if it was not too good for them, what makes us any different? Hell, we would not have half of the rights we have today if they had not protested. Black people seem to have been much stronger back then than we are now. Is this because we have gotten too comfortable? We need to get off our buttocks as a whole group and walk, March, and even run to make a positive stand for our race. If the dope man gets arrested, another dope man takes his place. If a black leader gets assassinated, no one is so quick to take his place. Rev. Dr. Martin Luther King Jr. once said, "A man who won't die for something is not fit to live." Come on, black people; you know the saying, "There are two things we must do: pay taxes and die," but I say we must pray and take action. Peace and much love to all of the black people of America. We need each other. Every other race helps its people first, and there is nothing wrong with that, and that is why we must do the same. God blessed America and "We the people" means every man on this earth; it just so happens to be written in the books of American history. Ha ha. Shut up, Little Richard; Wake up, Spike Lee. I am not scared to do what needs to be done. What needs to be done is that we need to have more love for our race first, then our country, and then the world. It must be in that order. The government should also help our country first then the world second. I am a disabled army veteran. I spent eighteen years with the army and five years with the post office. That is twenty three total years with the government, and I am only 39.

Ran In An Arizona Newspaper

No More Mace! No More Horses!

This Is A Response To The Incident At The 2005 M.L.K. Festival.

It was January 17, 2005—Martin Luther King Jr. Day. The celebration was coming to a close. I must admit that I had a great time. The entertainment was on point, and being around my peeps was refreshing. My friend and I were walking around, looking for familiar faces. I noticed the police on horses with helmets on and mace on their hips. This instantly reminded me of being on Mill Avenue in August of 1992. The Tempe police department used this tactic to clear the streets at 1:00 a.m. Well, I thought nothing more of this and continued to look around and was contemplating what I wanted to eat. Not more than a few minutes after we reached the south side of the park, we noticed people running.

If you could have seen the panic, fear, and confusion on these people's faces, you would have thought that Arizona was under attack. For real, though, you would have thought this was 9/11 all over again. I placed my friend behind a tree and immediately placed a call to her children to assure their safety. I looked at my watch and noticed that it was about 4:05 p.m. I thought to myself, they must be trying to clear the park.

I looked up again and noticed the police in the middle of the people spraying them with mace and directing them to one side of the park. They had little altercations, but who's to say that the actions of the police didn't spark some of them? If you were in a crowd and being pushed, shoved, and trampled, wouldn't you be angry? Why yeah! There was no riot, so why were riot tactics used for a non-riot situation? This action only caused negative reactions, which in turn sparked fear, panic, and confusion. There were people of all ages, from the elderly to babies, who could have been seriously hurt or even killed due to these tactics. If this had happened, it would not have been the first time. I was introduced to this tactic in 1992, and we are now in 2005—thirteen years later. Can we get a better technique? When are you going to learn? I guess, in your minds, you are thinking, why change a good thing? I know how Arizonans hate to be told what to do; therefore, consider this a reality check attached to a moral and conscious decision to do the right thing. With this in mind, I say (and please repeat after me): No more horses, no more mace, no more horses, no more mace; this is degrading to our race. No more horses and no more mace!

Thank you, and Godspeed.

www.boycottblackmen.com

Hello,

My name is Ryan E. Strickland; I am a proud man who happens to be black. I have, for the most part, always dated black women. My only two children are from the same black woman. We did not get married, but that was her choice. I have had three serious relationships, and they have been with black women. Either they wanted to wear the dress and the pants or they were too free with their bodies— free enough to get me a medal for bringing pussy to the troops. Excuse the language. I'm not a pimp, so I did not get paid and although I was a soldier, I didn't get my medal. All I did receive was harassment, embarrassment and a divorce. In spite of all of that, I still have not given up just yet. I have four beautiful black sisters, and they are good women. Therefore, I know I will someday be blessed with a black woman who will have my back as I will have hers. She will be faithful to me and me to her. We will be able to share our feelings, good and bad. We will make love to each other as if it was the first time. She will take care of me, and I will most definitely, without any hesitation, take care of her. There are many reasons people do not want to see black men with black women. One is *The Willie Lynch Letter and the Making of a Slave.* The other is that no matter what the black man does, he is still looked down upon. Even if the black man is rich and famous; it is like the world is waiting for him to mess up just so they can say "I told you so" or "I knew that 'N' was no different from the rest." Some might even say, "You can dress a nigger up, but only to play house, 'cause if you take that nigger out, he's gonna act a fool." Black sisters of America don't give up on us. Just give us the same guidance and chances you give white Americans, Asian Americans, and now Mexican Americans. Everyone is looking down on the black man although they want to be like the black man. You know what the next movie should be? "What Would America Be Like Without The Black Man?" That would be very interesting. Some might not say it, but that is their wish. Ladies, I have had it bad enough in my life without having to have this to deal with also. I have two Beautiful children, my daughter is six years old, and my son is five years old. I do not want them to go through the things I had to endure while growing up. White people did not like me because I was black. Black people did not like me because I was poor. If we do not stick together, then we will no longer exist. My book will be coming out as soon as I can get a publisher. The title: "Is Your Mind Shackle Free?" I think we should all ask ourselves this question. If all of you black women want to boycott the black man then is your mind shackle free? You know what would be nice is if you would just boycott the one who did you wrong. I have been the transitional man for two women for sure. I caught hell for whatever their ex-man did to them. That is no fun and you can do nothing right to please a woman who is still bitter with her ex-man. You can either date without getting serious or stay single until you are ready. Nevertheless, do not boycott the black man. We are not all messed up. I do not care if you make more money then me; just do not throw it up in my face to belittle me. Men have been the breadwinners in the household for years. Times change, and a different cycle has arisen. Another thing, not all black men get the same chances as the men in the other races. Teachers always challenge most black men. My son is only in kindergarten and his preschool teacher gave him negative marks when it came to his social skills. I was pissed about it, but his mother saw nothing wrong with it. They said that he was "too headstrong." I told them that is how I want him to be; he will need that in this world. I talked to him and explained that there is a time and place to use it and that I am very, very proud of him. My son—attacked at four years old. This is just an example of what we have to go through with people in this world. We should not have to take it from you too. We are all in the same house. It is us vs. everyone outside the house. That is what I tell my children. Stay blessed, and like Martin would say, "Stop; think about it."

Hello again,

The black man has always been talked about, negatively. If you all know a little black history you would see how the black woman was bred to be the stronger of the two people in the black race. In all of the other races the man is stronger. In America, what races have the most housewives? Think about it ladies before you jump out of your yard and into another. The black man has been put down throughout history. The black man has taken the fall for a lot of others' mistakes. The black man, unlike Lee Majors, is the real fall guy. Why don't you all write a book about the man who did you wrong and leave it at that? Most women have a much harder time getting over a relationship than men do. The reason for that is men have been bred to have no emotion. Let me say that again. Men have been bred to have no emotion. A white man will cheat on you. Hell, a white man will take an insurance policy out on you and kill you. Some will kill you just to be with a new female toy. All men have faults. The black race needs the most help right now. When a strong black woman and a strong black man, who are both used to being independent, develop a relationship, a power struggle is often created. This is why many of those relationships fail. Women, let the man be the man and men, let the woman be the woman. This does not mean cooking and cleaning. This duty should be shared in this time and age being that both people work. Once again in case no one caught that, both parents of a black family, for the most part, have to work if they are in the same household. This is not so common in the other races. The black woman is very strong, but so is the black man and that is why society feels that we are a threat. Moreover, what do they do with a threat? Kill us our lock us up. Why? They either want us to be silent, silenced, or repressed! This is no excuse, just facts. Once again, ladies—proud black women—I am Ryan Edward Strickland, and I am a strong, proud black man and I love my strong black women. Good luck on what you are trying to do. Just look at the big picture and not the heartbreaks. Black men need love too and lots of it. I do not know about all black men, although I do know this; I am not looking for a mother figure, I want a wife and business partner. For the record, all the Black men I know feel the same way I do about this. In my opinion, this is what a marriage is about. Consult one another and never cheat your relationship and you will prosper.

Peace,

Hello Everyone,

I have one for the books too. I feel that the problem lays in both people not just the man especially the Black Man. When we take a stand to do our job we are often resisted for doing so. Then if we fall short of doing a grand job we are quickly ridiculed. If we don't make enough money then most of the time we are unwanted by our own Black Women. If you stick by us we will stick by you. If you do not slander our names we will not slander yours. What we all need to realize here is this: The American System does not and has never wanted Black America to SUCCEED as a group! This is a known fact. We as Black Men & Women play their game to the fullest on the negative tip. Do you know what I mean? We play their game to the fullest by BREAKING UP OUR FAMILIES, HAVING TOO MANY RELATIONSHIPS, NOT COMMITING TO ONE PERSON! Which results in: Making too many babies! Men can't do this alone! Not to mention we are failing in EDUCATING OURSELVES AND EACH OTHER. We are falling short of taking our rightful spot in our household. First of all, we need a house of our own. The fact is that some of us are not sharing or being allowed to share the responsibility of having the bills in both of our names nor do some of you want this. (THIS IS VERY IMPORTANT!) Reason being both people are trying to establish credit. By having

Our Strong Black Women & the System Slander the Black Man's Image by saying things like The Black Man is a Worthless Lazy Bum who thinks the world owes him something. Plus, I must add the false presumption that we as Black Men are all deadbeat Dad's. When in reality, <u>half the time, **but not all of** the time</u>, the Black Woman only wants the child support and still prohibits the father from spending time with his children. What does this do for our children? Our children love both parents or would if they had the chance to know both parents? Some Black Men give up. Not me! I challenged that and won. Not only do I see my children on a regular basis. I talk to my children on a regular basis. Therefore, you know I must be taking care of my children. They have way more then I did. This should be our goal to see that this happens and their Birth Right. With this we should also explain so that they understand it does not have to be this way. It's just you want better for them because you may not have had this yourself growing up. Example: My son had his first suit when he was two years old. I had my first suit when I was 18 years old. You may like this or not. You may or may not believe what I'm about to say. Either way it is still a fact! Not an "Excuse!" The Black Man does have it harder than any other Man on this Earth. Anyone who addresses this has their own opinion and of course you know I have mine. You know what my answer is? "INTIMIDATION" America and most of the World is Intimidated by the Black Man. Reason being we are able to overcome many obstacles put before us which in return we produce great revenue. (That is to say, whenever we realize our full potential!) Now for the Black Men, we need not to Slander our Black Women's Image by calling her every name in the book, but her name given to her by her parents! When are we going to learn? We should not provoke one another. We should not beat one another. We desperately need to find solutions to our problems and not run from them. We should stop drinking and doing drugs to hide from them! If a problem goes unanswered it does not go away it gets bigger! Face it like you face the person you want to sleep with. We are all brave then. Besides, America Loves Sex. (Did you notice I said, America Loves Sex and not just Black People?) We are not over sexed like they claim. Pick up a newspaper to see if you see what I have seen? They put ads in the newspaper soliciting sex, (From Black People!) *Mental Note!* Back to my thoughts: Therefore face your problems like "YOUR ONE HORNY RABBIT!" *So to speak.* Maybe with this attitude we will be more productive on a positive tip. We also need to stop using each other! DO NOT HUSTLE EACH OTHER, BUT MAKE THE WORLD AND LIFE YOUR HUSTLE? However remain positive just like: Bill Cosby, Oprah Winfrey, Michael Jordan, Will Smith, Master P., Damon Dash and Jay Z.

One more thing Black People, we need to learn how to Love one another! Let's make a promise to each other: The Promise between The Strong Black Man "2" The Strong Black Woman "1"! This creates:

"The Strong, Beautiful, Black Couple"

I Promise you: <u>The One You Love:</u> I will refuse to Slander your Name or your Image! We will Love and Respect One Another. If you get sick or fall short of your norm I will help you up and guide you through your time of struggle. We will be one. Your goals will become my goal in order to help you achieve your goals. We will do our best not letting anyone come between us. Reason being, my Love and respect for you, plus your strength will not allow it. You are my light my love my every being. We are 2 but we are 1. Your thoughts are mine thoughts and my thoughts are yours. When we are married, and we start our family, we can sit back and view what our love and strengths has help us create. I Love you, I Will Honor and Respect your beliefs, I will listen to you whenever you wish to speak; my reasons are we are 2, but we are 1, and I Love you, My Strong Beautiful Black Love! We are, The Strong Beautiful Black Love! We are, The Strong Beautiful Black Couple! I wrote this some time ago to use as my Wedding Vows for the woman I was suppose to Marry.

Thank you,

My Response To 'Jena 6'

Hello Governor Blanco,

My name is Ryan E. Strickland. This incident is clearly a case of self-defense. It is a clear cut case , the Black students were merely defending themselves. Reason being, what the white kids did was a purposely well thought out HATE CRIME. Hands Down! This was a HATE CRIME! To make a hang noose in the United States is against the Law or at least is suppose to be. So I ask you this, since when is it a crime to defend yourself? The Black students did exactly what they are supposed to do. They protested the Hate Crime brought forth against them. Then they presented their case of facts through the proper channels. These actions in return got the proper attention of the appropriate authorities. However, the punishment brought forth was mild to none toward the white students for this Hate Crime! Also instead of this act of Hate Crime being highly enforced, it would not be tolerated; it seems to me that the white kids were commended. Otherwise they would not have continued to choose to torment the Black students. The laws that were put in place to protect all of America were not properly administered here. Instead it left the door wide open for the Black students to continue to be harmed in lieu of protected. What is wrong with this picture? This is indeed, without a doubt, an intentional, premeditated

HATE CRIME CASE Against Black People which is against our CIVIL RIGHTS as Americans. We as Americans are supposed to be protected under these laws set in place by the United States Government. Therefore I ask you again, why is it that these children are being punished for protecting themselves? It is very obvious that the law refused to protect them. Would you rather they be killed and their family protest their death? Make it FAIR! Make it Right! Because, the way this appears to the World, it is just "WHITE!" NOT RIGHT! My final questions to you Governor Blanco are as follows: Are we as Black America not suppose to defend ourselves against white America when they do us wrong? Are we only supposed to defend ourselves against Black America? Is this the message you want us to receive? Is this where you want our rights to end? I also like to know when all of this is going to end; the "Black vs. White, or White vs. Black thing? What is up? Please tell me, because, I'd....... like to do the right thing!

Thank you,

HIP HOP VS. AMERICA

OR IS IT AMERICA VS. HIP HOP

You know this is very interesting. Although I was born in the 60's I can still reflect back on history. It really wasn't that long ago, America vs. Rock & Roll. Does anyone remember that? If you think about it Rock & Roll wasn't really acceptable until Elvis came along. They went as far as placing tape down the middle of the dance floors just to separate the kids from one another. Now it is Hip Hop. When is America going to take blame for its part on corrupting America? I do not agree with everything Hip Hop brings to the table, but I have seen the good Hip Hop has done for all of The World. In my opinion, Hip Hop is today, what Rock & Roll was yesterday. Do you all know what I mean? Music is a very important part of our life. Music has catered to all of our needs at one time or another. My Examples: Good times, hard times, falling in Love, Making Babies. Most of us wouldn't be here if it wasn't for some type of music. Music also soothes in ability for getting over Heart Breaks; motivates you to start your day or to pursue a career. Furthermore and most importantly, it Bridges the Gap, bringing Unity within Different Worlds. In my opinion, what America wants the Hip Hop Artist to understand is that you have a great deal of power all at the tip of your verse? In my opinion, what the Hip Hop Artist wants America to understand is, we are products of our environment and are not all bad.

Plus if you listen to our music and not try to scrutinize it you will hear what we see. All Artists imitate life and we as people imitate art. That's just the way it goes. Both sides have a good argument. As far as Hip Hop goes this one question touches me deeply. The question came from my five year old son. My son asks me why do they say that word so much in their songs and I can't say it? *"You know tha- word."* I looked at him. I had to pull over. I really didn't know what to say at first. So my first response was, I do not know son. Then I said, maybe they get paid for saying it. My next response was a question for him. So I ask, do you hear Daddy saying the word. His reply was no. So I said, it doesn't matter if you hear someone else use it, if Daddy doesn't use it, you can't either. He replied, ok Dad. Now, as far as America goes, if we, Americans, can clean up America then the Hip Hop Artist would be able to clean up their music. It would be mighty hard to rap or sing about bad times or "F" the Police if you didn't encounter some sort of unwarranted mishap. In other words, you can't rap a bad verse if you are experiencing good times. We all know it is always easier to point the finger then to accept blame. Plus it is really easy to point the finger if you may have a lot to hide. The truth is we are all at fault here. The argument seems to be who is more wrong, which doesn't make since. We should try to correct ourselves first before we try to correct someone else. Plus, we should also not consider working together we should just do it. Being, both are very powerful organization instead of America vs. Hip Hop or Hip Hop vs. America, let's try, America & Hip Hop United. How about it? The duties of this organization will be to right a wrong; and to Educate America, so we all can experience the "GOOD LIFE" Kenya West and Ha Ha Ha Ha Ha "Straight to The Bank." Curtis "50 Cent" Jackson. This can have a very positive outcome and can become the new and improved **National Association for the Advancement of Colored People** NAACP, which should be the (**National Association for the Advancement of People** NAAP!) I am not a colored person. Are you? How about that? This is just something to think about coming from a concerned citizen. Furthermore, I like to add the real reason Hip-Hop is under attack is very obvious to me and should be to all of us. Does anyone want to take an Educational Guess? Well, to me it is very simple. The leaders in Hip-Hop are all Successful Black Men. To simplify this even further, basically, THERE IS NO ELVIS IN HIP-HOP! Point Blank! This is the answer cut & dry! You all know this. It just so happens to be the same affect Rock & Roll had on America when it was created. Now here we are again in full circle, the same leading faces, but with a New Style. Hip-Hop Artist are becoming, too *Influential,* too *Wealthy* and too *Black.* Is that an Oops? I think not, I said it! Plus they can't find their nitch to fit in, so for now they are behind the scene. They can't adapt. Hip-Hop keeps evolving rapidly. Everytime they get close something new happens in the Hip-

Hop Lifestyle. They are having a hard time finding their Elvis of Hip-Hop! Now do you see what I see?

I am the author of the soon to be released book "Is Your Mind Shackle Free?" This is the real question we should be asking ourselves. Everyone on the panel made a great point. Now, we have to find the solution that fits our race and our life style. One thing that is missing in the topic is this: a Black man in America has always been the scape goats for all negative acts committed in America. Even though everyone wants to be like him, they don't want to carry the burden of being the Black man. Black women **don't always;** *I didn't say ever. I said don't always,* respect us as their counterpart or better half unless we have a good job or we sell a hustle on the street. We are either too poor for the poor Black woman or we are too poor, too gangster and too uneducated for the upper-class Black woman. If we chose to step out of our race we get attacked or if we stick with our race we get attacked. The system attacks the Black man and no one pays attention to this and this bothers me! We are put down for bringing it to the attention. Now it is Hip Hop; Hip Hop is under attack and some of it should be, but who is behind it. Who is behind it and who is left to take the blame? Black men are in front and doing well, some are doing very well. Do they get credit for the positive? Hell NO! Why? Well, I will tell you why. It is still part of a plan to destroy the Positive image of the Black man! "WOW" Allow me to say that again, IT IS STILL PART OF A

PLAN TO DESTROY THE POSITIVE IMAGE OF THE BLACK MAN! What they don't show on regular TV is that most of the Hip Hop Artists are married with Families and they have College Degrees. Why won't they show this? Well, I gave you the answer twice and once in all capital letters.

This is the same system that wanted to say the Simpson's was more realistic then the "COSBY'S! Does anyone remember that? Do you even know why this was said? Do you even care? I care and this is why: The Cosby's, showed a traditional middle class Black/African American family. Some people felt this image was untraditional, but this opinion is merely based on where you are from and how you are raised. The Cosby's were a married couple, both with professional careers, Mrs. Cosby was a lawyer and Mr. Cosby was a Doctor. They also juggled the duties of being parents and were very good at it too. The Cosby's, displayed morals, great family values; and were raising their children to be just like them, positive and responsible. Similar to the Cleaver's, although Mrs. Cleaver was a homemaker/housewife and Mr. Cleaver, was the provider of the family or the bread winner. Both family's positive. Both families were trying to raise their children to be respectable citizens of the community. The only difference which is and was very obvious is the color of the family's skin. One more acceptable which appeared to be more realistic, the other appeared to be very rare which appeared to be more fictional. Which all stem behind the color of their skin? Some will still argue the point color doesn't matter. However, it is very clear to me that it really does. They don't ever want the Black man to bear a positive Image if this is the case we will have Black ruling the world and the system will do its' best to prevent that. Believe me when I say that there! WE, WE, WE, I AM NOT TRYING TO SPEAK FRENCH I AM MAKING A POINT: WE CAN AND WILL IF WE KEEP HAVE DISCUSSIONS LIKE THESE CHANGE OURSELVES FOR THE BETTER! Just like history repeats itself if you don't know it, life will evolve to become better if we seek it! Therefore we should listen to Prince. Prince has been saying for years to all Artists, which includes, Hip Hop and R&B, take control of your music. This is why he changed his name. He was in the middle of his evolution! Not many people caught that, some people just made fun of him instead. While you may laugh just to be laughing the Tha-Man is laughing at you because he knows the truth. Pay attention! Will Smith set a great example years ago with clean lyrics plus urged others to clean up their music and he came under attack by a white rapper. No one spoke up to defend Will. Even though he has helped many people at one time or another, by allowing them to appear on his hit TV show, "The Fresh Prince." Talk about biting off the hand that feeds you!" Where is his props plus respect? I can go on, but so can each and every one of us. So I am going to say this in closing; In order for us to better ourselves we only need to reach out to ourselves. We must reach out to ourselves so that we can ACCEPT OURSELVES, "US REACHING US PLUS US ACCEPTING US!" This is the most important deciding factor here!

I Am An Example

I am nothing but an example of what America has defined as a: Nigger, Negro, Nigga, Colored, Coon, Jigger Boo; African American Black Man. I have been through a lot of transformation in my 40 years of life. Some I could say brought me victories and some I can say brought me shame. Shame that was pretty much expected of me, but shame none-the-less I wish I could erase. I gave into what is expected of me by the world as a man of the underprivileged. Now that I am more aware of this I would be nothing other then a fool if I continued on that path and or also a **Charlatan** (hypocrite). I do not wish to continue to be an example of the negative perception of this man. What I wish and seek to become is a Proud Black American whom my children and family can look to with respect. I came from disrespect and shame to respect and personal victory. In closing I would like to say if I can overcome my obstacles of shame we all can overcome those types of obstacles. The power does not lie with the media we make the media what it is. The power does not lie in the world we make the world what it is. The power does however lie within us, us as Black/African Americans. We waywardly decide our outcome for not knowing the abundance of choices which are placed before us. Thus we realize that without knowledge of this system we will never succeed. Once we comprehend this system then and only then will we achieve success. Consequently we must seek what is rightfully ours and what is rightfully ours is information. With this gain of awareness we will without force fall into our perspective places. Such as in nature: as a tree looses a leaf it shall naturally fall to the ground. We as Black/African Americans shall fall into our ecosystem of knowledge? Believing this is our key to the locks of difficulty we face. This is a true statement.

THE QUESTION: SHOULD MARION JONES BE STRIPPED OF HER MEDALS?

My answer: No!
My Reasons:

In my opinion, Marion Jones, should not be stripped of her gold medals. They all knew. Believe that! If I was a betting person, I would put a million dollar bet on that. It's unfortunate for her to be one of the ones who got caught. Don't be fooled people! They all knew, plus they all had their hands in the *cookie jar*. In this situation and others like this someone has washed their hands like the Romans did in the case of Jesus. If you all believe that these athletes are doing this on their own, you are *blind*, *deaf*, and *dumb* or possibly all three and then some. There are always people behind the athlete, which, in my opinion, should be a Lifetime Movie **titled "The People Behind the Athlete."** How is that for a title? We need to WAKE THE HELL UP! Marion Jones was a product, a money *making product*! Now that she is no longer producing they want to hang her *black ass* out to dry or put her *black ass* out to *Pasteur*, so to speak. Look at the big picture. There is much more behind this story as well as every other one like it. Whether we are Athletes, Soldiers, or Cotton Pickers; we are either a product, have been a product, will be viewed as a product, or just used as a product. Regardless of how we are viewed, we have always been discarded when no longer able to produce. We are and will always be the fall guy unless we put a stop to it. I strongly feel when an athlete gets punished then whomever is behind the athlete should also receive punishment for their shared participation. This would bring balance to the whole situation, plus put a rapid end to the usage of any altering/enhancing drugs. If all are brought forward and punished then all is resolved, which will be the end of the problem! Wouldn't you agree?

Thank you,

QUESTIONS YOU SHOULD ASK YOURSELF

Now, tell me this: Do you feel that *The Willie Lynch Letter and the Making of a Slave* still affects us today? Ask yourself these questions and answer them as they apply to you personally. I would like for you to really pay close attention and think about each one. This is your time to evaluate yourself. So if you do not answer honestly you are only cheating yourself. The only one who will know the answer to these questions is you.

1) Have you ever seen two beautiful Black/African American women, one a red bone and the other savory chocolate, and chosen the red bone?

2) Have you ever seen someone in your race who you felt was not on your level, so you belittled him or her?

3) Have you ever had an old relative that you knew was too old or sick to take care of himself or herself, but instead of bringing the relative to your house, you left him or her in their house or put them in an old folks' home?

4) Do you want to be successful but are afraid to achieve the success?

5) Do you not trust or envy your brother for his accomplishments? Do you trust or praise Tha-Man?

6) Do you feel that marriage is not and never will be, for you?

7) Have any of you brothers denied your child when you knew that the baby was yours?

8) Have any of you brothers turned your back on your children and not even looked back?

9) Have any of you sisters turned your backs on your children or left your parents to raise them?

10) Have any of you sisters ever become pregnant by a brother just to keep him?

11) Have any of you sisters ever told a brother that he was the father of your child when you knew darn well he was not?

12) Have any of you sisters run to the system first before even trying to work things out with a brother? Or held the child as leverage against the father?

13) Do you brothers try to help the sisters out financially so they do not have to depend on the system?

14) Do you sisters place unnecessary restraining orders against a brother, knowing that the law will believe you first?

15) Have any of you brothers ever disrespected a sister and called her out of her name?

16) Have any of you sisters ever disrespected a brother and called him out of his name?

17) Have any of you sisters had a brother who had positive goals, but because you did not believe in his goals, you put him down and provided no moral support?

18) Have any of you brothers had a sister who had positive goals, but because you did not believe in her goals, you put her down and provided no moral support?

19) Do any of you sisters think that you are just too independent for a brother and are your favorite saying, "I don't need a man?"

20) Do you know of or are you yourself a single parent or do you come from a single-parent home?

21) Are any of you brothers in on the Down-Low Club?

22) Are you sisters being like the Jones's or is this your lifestyle?

23) Have you been in a situation in which you or someone you know was discriminated against, but you did nothing about it because you felt that it would not change anything?

24) Have you ever or do you now hold a position at your job though you have the experience to have a higher position? Will they not promote you or give you a raise, but give you many duties due to your ability in order to save the company money? Though both you and they know that you are capable and worthy of the promotion and the raise, do you refuse to say anything about it to avoid conflict?

25) Do you keep a budget?

26) Do you live paycheck to paycheck?

27) Do you watch your credit report?

28) Do you know how to read your credit report?

29) Do you pray for opportunity without trying to make an opportunity happen?

30) Are you just a negative person who thinks that no matter what you do, things will never change?

31) Do any of you just outright dislike or hate yourself and your race?

Hustler: To act or appear to act quickly and forcefully in getting things done.

Tycoon: An important person in a specified business or industry.

Damon Dash's show was titled "The Ultimate Hustler?" When Donald Trumps show was titled "The Apprentice?"

32) Do you consider yourself a Hustler?

33) Would you rather be considered a Tycoon?

34) As Black American and African Americans why are we always considered to be a Hustler's? We are either successful in our fields or trying to become successful.

35) A friend of mine asks me, what type of crime determines if a person or group would be or should be considered a terrorist? I had to say good question. I personally feel anyone who consciously commits a crime of hate against a person should fall into this category. What do you think?

36) Can you answer this question?

37) Have you ever heard of a Black Hate Group?
Tick….tock….tick….tock…tick…..tock…….
Buzzzzzzzzzzzzzzzzz………

That's funny huh? I couldn't think of one either.

Although, I do know that some schools in America consider the Black Panther Party to be a Hate group, trouble makers and a group of people who they feel may have possibly committed treason.

If the teacher's who are teaching this would do some research they would reconsider that.

The Black Panther Party was a voice for the people. They studied the constitution and exercised their rights. Which in return they were severely punished, (Beaten), Incarcerated, and in some cases killed for doing so. One of their most famous stands that I recall reading about is when they realized they had the right to bear arms. This in return has been exercised by many since then. Although now, the government is reviewing this bill to determine if we are responsible enough to continue to exercise this right.

Well all I can say is, you decide. Do your own research and you determine who The Black Panther Party was?

We as Black/African Americans for the most part have always accepted all people, Regardless of race, gender, religion or sexual preface.

38) Why doesn't anyone accept us?

Please answer this for me.

Last but not least:

39) Do you think "The American Dream" is intended for only White/Caucasian people or do you think "The American Dream" is truly intended for anyone who lives in America?

Bonus:

40) In America if other races are to breed with the Black/African American Race, the off springs of this union are considered Black/African American. Now with this being the case, what would this make us; the minority or the majority?

Excluding question 40; If you answered yes to any of these questions do you feel it is possible that Willie Lynch has accomplished his goal? I know that I am guilty of some of these things myself, and I am the author. I also know that I am not alone. Especially since, I am not in this world alone. I must also add that a lot of this is us not knowing. Reason being, we are unaware or so use to what has happen to us that it has become our norm. In other words if we do not know what is wrong it will feel right if we have no truth to compare it to. Which brings me to this, it still boils down to one thing. The one thing is simple, but powerful and the answer is…."Knowledge" (WOW)! It is time for us to open our eyes. It is time for us to really see what they did and is still doing to us today no matter how moderate it may be. Just about all of us recognize when something is wrong and we think about what will make it right. We may not always act on our thoughts, but if it will bring about positive change we need to. It is the duty of us all to correct what is wrong. If we do nothing then we ourselves are wrong and we should not complain. We need to make our stand to be seen and heard once and for all. Everytime we do something that falls along the lines of the above questions we fall victim and begin attacking ourselves. This act will help Willie Lynch keep his dream alive. Therefore, we must put his dream to sleep as if it were a horse which has gone mad! We must all realize that it is indeed our time and there is no time like the present! Unite! This is an urgent and crucial matter that needs to be addressed! This does affect our existence! My Uncle Charles use to say "The party's over!" However, I am saying to all of my brothers and sisters, "The party has just begun!"

If you are one who does not accept change very well then maybe you should stay in the house or better yet stay in bed. Whether you recognize it or not, every day brings us change; yet somehow you manage to adapt. Go figure.

Now ask yourself again: Do you feel that the Willie Lynch experiment is still affecting us today? Hmmm. . .....

CHECKING OURSELVES TO BETTER OURSELVES

Now, with all these factors in mind let us realize that we must also be responsible for our own actions. Most of us have seen *New Jack City*. Some of us wanted to be Neno Brown (a drug dealer), but ended up being more like Pookie (a crackhead). The reason I say this is to give you this visual. Remember Pookie's famous crack scene. Pookie struggled with the crack, but in the end the crack won. Now consider yourself Pookie and consider the crack to be your finger. Do you understand? In other words, point your finger at yourself sometimes. Not all of the time, but sometimes. There is nothing wrong with this. There is even a name for it. It is called self evaluation. Besides, who would you rather correct you? Would you rather correct yourself or would you rather have someone else correct you? We as Black/African American men and women need to take responsibility for our own actions and not look for sympathy. Three-hundred years has passed. If sympathy did not reach you by now it's not going to. I do not know about you, but I surely do not want any sympathy. Do you? We should also accept what we can change and come up with a solution for what we cannot change. For the record, I know that some of us do this, but once again not all of us do. Until all of us are capable of doing this our chain will continue to contain a weak link. Once we are able to unite without violence, plus hatred, then and only then will we truly conquer and break free of the shackles on our minds.

Also, why is it that we as the Black/African American Man can only get credit for our wrong doings? There are a whole lot of us who do the right things in life, but we cannot get out of the shadow of the ones who don't. We need to be given credit for more than just the negative things in life. If we are not, we must demand it, but in a nonviolent manner. Furthermore, if the ones of us who are doing the right things get recognized for it then maybe the ones who are not will try to follow suit? Glorify our right doings instead of our wrong and see what happens. "Don't be scurrd!" If we follow our faith and remain positive, we can truly overcome all obstacles. We can regroup, unite, and never give up. Remember, if our ancestors can break the physical shackles, we can break the mental shackles.

I Am Tired

I am tired. I am tired of saying I am going to do something and then fail to do it. I am tired of hearing people complaining about things, especially when they are not trying to change them. What is it? Do you not have the courage or maybe you're sick, sick with a case of the lazes?

I am also tired of hearing about the black man who is not doing the right thing. In or about 1952 there was an article published in a newspaper. I did not see the article, but the information was passed down to me. It showed a white business man up front and a white hippie to his right. Then it showed a black blue collar working man behind them and a black bum to his right. The caption below the white business man read: ***"I am not responsible for his actions!"*** The caption below the black blue collar man read: **"Then why am I responsible for his?"** I share that to say this: We are placed in one category intentionally or unintentionally, both by society and by ourselves. We tend speak a lot about what the black man does not do. When in reality, we should redirect that energy toward what the Black men does do. I know if we focus on the Black Men who are doing the right things instead of focusing on the black men who are not then this will cause them to do right in life.

I am tired of people who are trying to make a difference and not receiving the support from our people to make those things happen.

I am proud of Dr. Martin Luther King Jr., but I am tired of hearing about his dream. I mean no disrespect. It just seems to me that American History only wants to remind us of only one Black Man's Dream; as if he was the only Black in the history of the world who had a dream. If this was the case then that would make him a freak of nature. Well, we all know that he was not a freak of nature. We all knew him to be a great man who got the job done with the support of others. Besides if he was a freak of nature, do you know what that would make the rest of us? That would make us (**"A No-Bo-dy, A Nobody!"**) I want to believe that if Dr. Martin Luther King Jr. was alive today he would tell us this same thing. My questions I ask you are: Do you need someone to think for you? Do you need someone to lead you around? Do you yourself dream? I dream. The way I see it, if we do not act on our dreams, this is disrespect. This is disrespect to not only Dr. Martin Luther King Jr., but to all Black/African Americans whose blood was shed for doing the right thing. I also feel, we should not allow others to make us feel bad for being proud of whom we are. We are the only race that gets criticized for being proud of who we are. I am very tired of that! Raise your fist. Be proud of who you are. Be very proud! Keep your fist raised. Now, place your left hand across your heart and make the peace sign. Remember, Pride is in our spirit; so be proud of who you are. Peace is in our hearts; never allow anyone to steal your peace. This way they cannot complain nor give any excuses. Most importantly they have to listen. If they do not listen it will make them look bad. Believe you me; they do not want to look bad. **(Live Your Dream!) We are all leaders if we choose to be!** Therefore you must: **Make your dreams your legacy!**

MY FINAL THOUGHTS

I have been working on my book for a very, very long time now and it is now 2007. I have recently seen a movie titled *The Pursuit of Happyness*. This movie is based on the true life story of Chris Gardner. First, I would like to say that the entire movie was good. For me, the part that meant the most was the end. I am not speaking about when they call him into the room and offered him a position. I mean the very end. To be exact the scene in which, Will and his son are walking and the actors pass the real Chris Gardner. The way Chris Gardner walks across the screen, sparked a very haunting and yet reviving feeling inside of me. He was there, but he was not there. I thought to myself, *it must really be nice to be able to possess that stroll of confidence!* I also thought about how nice it would be if we could all possess this quality!

Although there comes a time when we as Black/African Americans cannot always point the finger at the System, White people, They, Tha-man, or Anyone else. Reason being people died for us to have the things we are enjoying today. People died for us to excel beyond limits they only hoped and dreamed of or in some cases couldn't even imagine. People died for us to become great leaders and scholars. People died for us to be free. So regardless of how fair or unfair the system or people of the world may be; we still have things a Hell of a lot better then our people before us. This is why it is our responsibility to soar to a higher level of achievement and who ever should follow us must take it even further. I am going to leave you with this from the movie pride: "You are your own worst enemy. You got so much potential, but you ain't gonna do none of it because you won't get out of your own way." Jim Ellis

This is true. Reason being, at times we are our own worst enemy. Although with a whole lot of work we can change this. So please consider this work is nothing compared to what our ancestors had to bear. Please, please, remember, this the next time you want to quit on your family, your employment or a personal goal you have set for yourself. Our ancestors could not quit no matter how much they wanted too. At least today because of their efforts and Bloodshed, we have that choice.

To all Americans: We can only depend on the government to a certain degree. The government is busy? Therefore, we have to help ourselves as well as each other. In other words while the government is lending a helping hand to other countries, we as Americans have no choice, but to help one another. This is the only way we are truly going to make it.

Everything I have shared with you is important to me, but there is one other issue I would like for you all to think about. If you are not disabled, or if you do not have anything physically, or mentally, wrong with you and you are looking for a handout, think about this; "When you are given a handout the person giving determines how much you get but if you earn your own living, you determine!"

Now ask yourself, "Is My Mind Shackle Free?"
Remember, this is not a riddle!

Thank you,

Peace,
And May God, continue to bless you abundantly!

References

The Willie Lynch Letter and the Making of a Slave
By William Lynch
Published by Lushena books, February 1999, Second
Printing August 1999
"Provided by Internet Information"
Claiming to be Maya Angelou 2005 has not been
proven to be Maya Angelou!

Famous Black Quotations
Edited, selected, and compiled by Janet Cheatham
Bell
Warner books
Ref World Book 2002
Ref World Book G
The World Book Dictionary L-Z

New Jack City: DVD. Directed by Mario Van Peebles
Jacmac Films, 1991

The Feast of All Saints: DVD. Directed by Peter
Medak
Showtime Network Inc, 2003.

The Pursuit of Happyness: DVD. Directed by Gabriele
Muccino
Overbrook Entertainment, 2007.
Pride: DVD Directed by Sunu Gonera

Lions Gate Films, 2007
Eugene Thomas courtesy of Morning Business

The Steve Harvey Morning Show and Website. What was printed on Steve Harvey's website does not mean he agrees with my opinion or is he a supporter. He is excluded from any repercussions from my writings.

CENTER FOR DISEASE CONTROL CDC: has a website: www.cdc.com
PLAN PARENTHOOD 1-800-230-7526
ARIZONA COUNTY HOSPITAL STD'S DEPARTMENT
602-506-1678

Is Your Mind Shackle Free? Consists of my life experiences; observations, opinions, with the assumptions; that the Willie Lynch slave-breaking process is still affecting us today. With all of this in mind, I offer some solutions with questions which will allow you to think. In return, this will give you another perspective from which to view our world. This will permit you to evolve some of your own answers and questions. Then maybe we will all be on the same page and truly be able to view what has been and is still being done to us today.

Very Interesting Movies And Books:

I have seen all of these movies at least twice. I have read some of these books, and the ones I have not read yet are on my list of books to read.

Movies:
The Spook Who Sat By the Door: by Melvin Clay and Sam Greenlee

The Feast of All Saints: based on the book by Anne Rice

New Jack City: Giant Records/Warner Bros. Entertainment Inc.

Books:
The Willie Lynch Letter and the Making of a Slave
By Willie Lynch
Published by Lushena Books

Cool Pose: The Dilemmas of Black Manhood in America
By Richard Majors and Janet Mancini Billson

The Destruction of Black Civilization: Great Issues of a Race From 4500 B.C. TO 2000 A.D.
By Chancellor Williams

The Mis-Education of the Negro
By Carter G. Woodson

Narrative of the life of Frederick Douglass, an American Slave:
Written by Frederick Douglass & Introduced by Henry Louis Gates, Jr.

Countering the Conspiracy to Destroy Black Boys
By Jawanza Kunjufu

The Joshua-MEN-tality
By Rod Dillon

They Stole It but You Must Return It
By Richard Williams, Ed. D.

The Tuskegee Airmen Story (A Speech Guide) By The Speakers' Editorial Committee East Coast Chapter, Tuskegee Airmen, Inc.
HUNG: A Meditation On The Measure Of Black Men In America
By Scott Poulson-Bryant

Famous Black Quotations
By Janet Cheatham Bell

Fatherhood
By Bill Cosby, Introduction and Afterword by Alvin F. Poussaint, M.D.

A Child Shall Lead Them
By Bishop Alexis Thomas

Sins of The Father
By Felicia Madlock

Single, Saved, and Having Sex
By Ty Adams, foreword by Dr. Myles Munroe

*Black Wall Street: From Riot to Renaissance in Tulsa's
Historic Greenwood District*
By Hannibal B. Johnson

The Isis Papers: The Keys to The Colors
By Dr. Frances Cress Welsing

*Black Spark, White Fire: Did African Explorers
Civilize Ancient Europe?*
By Richard Poe, foreword by Dr. Molefi Kete Asante

About Me

Hello America,

I did not have a good life growing up. I know America is tired of black men saying this. Well, in my case this is the truth. In my past I had allowed my situation and people to anger me. My anger has held me from progressing in some areas of my life and also caused me some untraceable health problems. (**Stress**) At one point of my life anger had almost cost me my freedom. Looking back, I realize, I was nothing but a product of my environment, one could even say a puppet of my environment. Some of you may say Bull****. You are using this as an excuse for your failures or lack of progression. I'm telling you no. Hell no! This is not an excuse. This is the truth and I will tell you why. I was a victim of my environment along with being a puppet; not really by choice, but unfortunate circumstance and subconsciously by comfort. Do you understand? Allow me to explain a little more. Although I did not like my situation or some of the people I was around, I was comfortable. I was comfortable because this was all I was familiar with. This created a cushion of comfort for me which blocked my vision or dreams. How many of you go outside your familiar or comfort zone? Are you with me? Let's continue. I also could not see past my anger. I always felt like something was wrong, but being angry clouded my thoughts and sometimes my judgment. Now please understand, I did not walk around angry all day, nor did I have a chip on my shoulder, waiting for someone to try to knock it off. No, it wasn't even like that. I would get angry instead of getting depressed. I would get angry if I felt I was being attacked. Are you with me? Anger was like a burglar alarm you use to give you your piece of mind in your homes. My anger, in my mind was my protection from my environment, but it also blocked me from seeing a better life. If it wasn't for God's placement of certain people in my life, along with a reality check and perhaps the military; I would have easily become a statistic. Thanks to Anger Management Class, I now realize my anger stemmed from ignorance. In hindsight, anger was not my friend, but my closest enemy. I say that to say this, without much of an education, self-control, and awareness, I would act in the only way I knew; which in my case was street survival. Don't be mistaken, there are many different types of street survival. I was around drug dealers, but they never taught me the game. They pushed me down a different path, plus this was never in my goals or dreams anyway. I never robbed anyone or anything like that. I earned my way. Some may consider it the hard way, but honest way. I washed dishes, sold cans, threw news papers, dabbed a little in asbestos removal. I worked construction, fast foods, grocery stores, clothing stores, cleaned carpets. I also worked in nursing homes, and I was even a door to door salesman. I sold a multipurpose cleaner called Advantage for A & W Enterprises. Some may say a jack of all trades and a master of none. I call it trying my darnedest to survive. Now, I am striving to reach a new level of success. I wish to obtain a college degree. Which will be a more manageable and respectable style of success. I will still act against any wrong doings. However, without anger, but with calm wisdom. I still struggle in some areas from time to time, but now I am more aware, calm and a little bit wiser. I am hoping my message is understood and respected. You will hear from me again. My next book is going to reflect my evolution of self-improvement. This is a promise. I have a good re-pore with my children when it comes to keeping my promises and I hope to do the same with you as readers.

I was born, March 24, 1967. I was raised in a home with mostly women. My mother was a single parent, who worked as a caretaker, maid and various other jobs to support or family. We even contributed as recipients to the government's financial system.... (a.k.a. welfare). She raised seven children, four daughters and three sons. I am an identical twin. Although my twin did not survive, his spirit and presence has and always will be with me. Knowing I am a twin; gives me an extra drive to become successful. I am a proud father of two children, one girl and one boy. I have tried my share of careers. My main goal in mind is to show the younger people in my family that if you never give up, you can do anything you set your mind too. I served a total of 18 years in the military and attended several colleges, while serving our country. Immediately after my Honorable Discharge from the Military, I was a Corrections Officer and a Certified Instructor. I was given the opportunity to model locally, which leads to acting positions. I was an extra in Jane Seymour's movie, Sun Stroke, and had a bit part in a Billy Blank's movie, Showdown. (I catch a beat down. Funny scene though, plus it $PAID WELL! YEP!) I am the type of person who faces my mistakes and issues straight on and some people are not use to this method. We all have issues and will make mistakes, it is apart of life. However, should we allow this to stop us from success? NOPE! All of this is a part of what is to be considered our growth period. This is supposed to help mold us into who we become. When we make it, there are too many of us who like to hoard information which can be very useful to others in reaching their goals. If the knowledge will help out a brother, then pass it on. Some might say, "If I can make it, then so can you!" This is not always so. Therefore, we need to teach each other what we know, so that our race can mature and prosper. For the last time, we must push the crabs out of the barrel instead of pulling them back down. Who knows, one day the crabs who makes it out of the barrel just may lend you a claw. In 1987, I attended Basic Training. My Drill Sergeants had me recite this; "Good Better Best, Never Let Me Rest, UNTIL My Good Is Good and My Betters Best!" I am not sure where they got this, but I still remember it. I also try to live by it. Peace and Prosperity is what I wish for all of us in America and the World!